SCHOLAR Study Guide

CfE Advanced Higher Biology
Unit 2: Organisms and Evolution

Authored by:

Bryony Smith (North Berwick High School)

Dawn Campbell (Falkirk High School)

Reviewed by:

Fiona Stewart (Perth Grammar School)

Previously authored by:

Jaquie Burt

Lorraine Knight

Eileen Humphrey

Nadine Randle

Heriot-Watt University

Edinburgh EH14 4AS, United Kingdom.

First published 2015 by Heriot-Watt University.

This edition published in 2015 by Heriot-Watt University SCHOLAR.

Copyright © 2015 SCHOLAR Forum.

Distributed by the SCHOLAR Forum.

SCHOLAR Study Guide Unit 2: CfE Advanced Higher Biology

1. CfE Advanced Higher Biology Course Code: C707 77

ISBN 978-1-909633-61-2

Printed and bound by CPI Group (UK) Ltd, Croydon, CR0 4YY

Acknowledgements

Thanks are due to the members of Heriot-Watt University's SCHOLAR team who planned and created these materials, and to the many colleagues who reviewed the content.

We would like to acknowledge the assistance of the education authorities, colleges, teachers and students who contributed to the SCHOLAR programme and who evaluated these materials.

Grateful acknowledgement is made for permission to use the following material in the SCHOLAR programme:

The Scottish Qualifications Authority for permission to use Past Papers assessments.

The Scottish Government for financial support.

The content of this Study Guide is aligned to the Scottish Qualifications Authority (SQA) curriculum.

Contents

Topic 1

Field techniques for biologists

Contents

Prerequisite knowledge

You should already know that:

- *risk assessments are performed prior to experimentation, outlining safety precautions;*

- *life can be classified into the three domains: bacteria, archaea and eukaryotes;*

- *animals can be tracked using banding, ringing, tagging and satellite transmitters;*

- *ethology is the study of animal behaviour, and that observations are recorded on an ethogram.*

Learning objectives

By the end of this topic, you should be able to:

- *state some hazards and risks associated with field work;*
- *explain that working in the field may have a greater range of hazards than working in the laboratory;*
- *describe appropriate methods for sampling wild organisms;*
- *explain what random, systematic and stratified mean in reference to sampling;*
- *name methods used in the identification of living things;*
- *state the major divisions in both the plant and animal kingdoms;*
- *explain that monitoring populations can provide important information for assessing environmental impact;*
- *describe the method of mark and recapture in estimating population size;*
- *give examples of effective and ethical methods of marking;*
- *state how animal behaviour is measured and recorded.*

1.1   Health and safety

All practical work, whether in a laboratory or in the field, involves identification of the hazards and risks involved. A risk assessment is a document that identifies the potential hazards, assesses the likelihood of them occurring and clearly describes the steps that can be taken to minimise their occurrence, therefore reducing the possibility of injury or loss. The risk assessment will also outline who is most at risk from the identified hazards. Fieldwork may involve a wider range of hazards compared with working in the laboratory. Additional hazards and risks associated with fieldwork include:

- **terrain** - refers to how the land lies. Variations in terrain may include uneven surfaces, flat areas, hills and steep gradients. Assessing this prior to setting out and selecting appropriate footwear is essential;

- weather conditions - these can change very quickly in the field. A weather forecast should be consulted before setting out, and appropriate clothing, footwear and supplies selected. In extreme weather, fieldwork may have to be postponed or abandoned;

- isolation - areas where fieldwork is carried out can often be isolated. Making sure that others who are not going into the field are aware of the route and the expected time of return is essential;

- tidal changes - these can change very quickly. Tide tables should be consulted prior to setting out.

1.2   Sampling of wild organisms

Sampling should be carried out in a manner that minimises impact on wild species and habitats. Consideration must be given to rare and vulnerable species and habitats which are protected by legislation. Since legislation may change with regional areas, these should be researched prior to beginning sampling.

Sampling techniques

Transect studies

A transect is a line along which different samples can be taken. These are often set up along an area where the terrain or abiotic factors are changeable, e.g. from a woodland into a field or up a sandy shore from the waterline to the high tide line. Abiotic factors may be sampled, as can plant abundance and the abundance of sessile, or very slow moving, organisms. Quadrats of a suitable size and shape for the area are placed along the transect, allowing organism abundance to be recorded. Meters are then used to measure the relevant abiotic factors, e.g. moisture, light, pH and salinity.

Point count

Point count is a sampling technique used in sampling bird populations in a given area over a set period of time. Counts are carried out by recording all birds seen and heard from a stationary point. Comparisons can be made throughout the year.

Remote detection

Remote detection employs the use of camera traps that are triggered when wildlife is present. This means that species that are more elusive, i.e. those that are difficult to find, can be observed without the observer being present.

Another good technique for elusive species is scat sampling, which is an indirect method whereby animal droppings are collected in particular areas, providing information about species abundance and diet.

There are different sampling techniques. These include random, stratified and systematic. It is important that the scientist selects the most appropriate method for the area and species being sampled.

- **Random sampling** - individuals selected from the larger population must be chosen completely by chance.

- **Stratified sampling** - in some cases, one large population may be divided up into smaller sub-populations first. Individuals are then randomly selected from each sub-population.

- **Systematic sampling** - may be taken at regular intervals, e.g. every 2 metres along the transect.

Go online

Sampling of wild organisms: Questions

A quadrat 50 cm long was used to sample the number of seaweed plants at five places along two different **line transects** on the rocky shore at South Queensferry. Quadrats were placed every 3 m along each. The results are shown in the following table.

Quadrat number	Number of seaweed plants	
	Area 1	*Area 2*
1	28	15
2	18	15
3	40	43
4	18	32
5	11	15

Q1: What is the mean density per square metre of Area 1?

. . . .

Q2: What is the mean density per square metre of Area 2?

. . . .

Q3: Explain why this is an example of systematic sampling.

. . . .

1.3 Identification and taxonomy

Identification of a sample can be made using expertise, classification guides, keys or laboratory analysis of DNA (including mitochondrial and chloroplast DNA), protein or other molecules, such as carbohydrates.

Life is generally classified according to relatedness. Being familiar with **taxonomic** groupings allows predictions and inferences to be made between the biology of an unknown or lesser-known organism and better-known (model) organisms. Model organisms are those that scientists already know a lot about and have been studying for many years. Organisms such as *E. Coli, drosophila,* yeast, maize, mice and zebra finches are all good examples of model organisms from different taxonomic groups. Sometimes, organisms may appear more or less related than they actually are due to convergent and divergent evolution respectively. Genetic evidence is often used to dispel myths regarding relatedness. It was recently used to show that red pandas are more closely related to racoons rather than the former theory, which suggested greater relatedness to the giant panda.

Red panda

Giant panda

Racoon

Life is classified into three domains.

1. Archaea

2. Bacteria

3. Eukaryota

The plant kingdom has major divisions such as:

- **mosses** - flowerless plants which lack seeds and a vascular system;

Moss covered forest floor

- **liverworts** - flowerless, spore-producing plants with flattened stems and overlapping leaves;

Liverwort by https://commons.wikimedia.org/wiki/User:Avenue, licenced under the https://en.wikipedia.org/wiki/en:GNU_Free_Documentation_License

- **ferns** - flowerless plants that reproduce by producing spores and which have a vascular system;

Green fern

- **gymnosperms** - flowerless plants that produce seeds for reproduction and which have a vascular system, e.g. the conifer;

Example of a gymnosperm - seeds are found in cones

- **angiosperms** - flowering plants.

Angiosperm - pansy

The animal kingdom is divided into phyla which include:

- **chordata** - the sea squirts and vertebrates, e.g. birds, mammals, reptiles, amphibians and fish;

Red spotted sea squirt at Windmill Beach on the Cape Peninsula by http://commo ns.wikimedia.org/wiki/User:Pbsouthwood, licenced under the Creative Commons http://creativecommons.org/licenses/by-sa/3.0/deed.en license

- **arthropoda** - the joint-legged invertebrates which are identified by their segmented body, typically with paired appendages, e.g. wasps, butterflies, spiders and crabs;

Arthropod - monarch butterfly

- **nematoda** - the round worms which show great variety, many of which are parasitic, e.g. tapeworms;

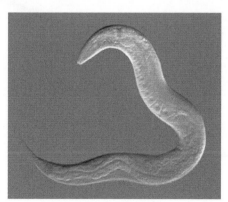

Nematode C. Elegans by http://bio.unc.edu/people/faculty/goldstein/, licenced under the Creative Commons https://creativecommons.org/licenses/by-sa/3.0/de ed.en license

- **platyhelminthes** - the flatworms, many of which are parasitic, show bilateral symmetry, lack a body cavity, but do contain internal organs;

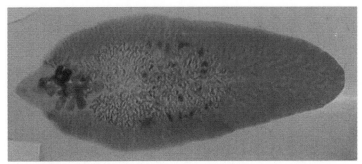

Fasciola hepatica - parasitic liver fluke, member of the platyhelminthes

- **mollusca** - the molluscs which are greatly varied, with many characterised by the presence of a shell, e.g. snails and octopi.

Mollusc - snail

Identification and taxonomy: Activity

Q4: Match the taxonomic groups with their definitions.

Go online

Angiosperm:	non-flowering, seed producing vascular plant such as a conifer.
Anthropods:	flowerless plant that produces spores and has a vascular system.
Chordata:	parasitic flatworms.
Fern:	parasitic roundworms.
Gymnosperm:	animal group containing sea squirts and vertebrates.
Moss:	flowering plants.
Molluscs:	invertebrates with jointed pairs of legs and segmented bodies.
Nematodes:	invertebrate group often found to have a shell.
Platyhelminthes:	flowerless plant, lacking both seeds and a vascular system.

. . . .

1.4 Monitoring populations

Monitoring populations is essential in understanding environmental conditions. Presence, absence or abundance of particular indicator species can give information of environmental qualities, such as the presence of pollutants. For example, biodiversity of lichen species in an area can indicate the levels of sulphur dioxide in the air. Likewise, freshwater invertebrates are frequently used to indicate sewage pollution.

Mark and recapture is a method for estimating population size. A sample of the population is captured, marked and released (M). The marking technique used must have minimal impact on the species being studied, thus does not interfere with the individual's normal behaviour or make it more conspicuous to predators. It must, however, also be clear in order to permit subsequent observations. After an interval of time, a second sample is captured (C). If some of the individuals in this second sample are recaptures (R), then an estimate of the total population (N) would be calculated using the formula:

$$N = \frac{MC}{R}$$

- N = estimate of total population;
- M = number captured, marked and released in first sample;
- C = number captured in second sample;
- R = number of marked recaptures in second sample.

Several assumptions are made when using this equation:

- all individuals have an equal chance of capture;
- there is no immigration of emigration during the sample time;
- there is no birth and death during the sample time;
- sampling methods used each time are identical.

Methods of marking include banding, tagging, surgical implantation, painting and hair clipping.

Snail marked and released

Go online

Monitoring populations: Question

Q5: In a survey to estimate a monarch butterfly population in Strathclyde Park, the following data were obtained.

- Number of monarch butterflies first captured, marked and released = 540
- Number of marked monarch butterflies in second capture = 60
- Number of unmarked monarch butterflies in second capture = 180

Calculate the estimated population of monarch butterflies in Strathclyde Park.

. . . .

1.5   Measuring and recording animal behaviour

Ethology is the study of animal behaviour. An **ethogram** is a recording of all of the observed behaviours shown by a species over a particular period of time. Observed behaviours are recorded as descriptions, e.g. eating, head up, lying down, tail wagging, rather than by trying to infer what the intention of the behaviour may be, e.g. displaying happiness.

The following is an example of an ethogram for an African wild dog.

Behaviour	Description
Resting	Lying on the ground / inactive.
Bow	Head lowered, sometimes front legs lowered too.
Tail wagging	Tail moving from side to side (usually horizontal or higher).
Tail lowered	Tail below horizontal, at times between back legs.
Feeding and drinking	Consuming food or water.
Standing alert	Standing still, looking in direction of movement or noise.
Sniffing ground	Head lowered and nose to the ground in exploration.

Ethogram for an African wild dog

It is essential that descriptions are clear and unambiguous. Extreme care must be taken to avoid **anthropomorphism** (personification), which is when animals are credited with human emotions and qualities.

Ethologists take measurements such as latency (the time taken for the animal to respond to a particular stimulus), frequency and duration of certain behaviours and activities. A time budget can be constructed using this data, which is the percentage of time that the animal spends on certain activities.

Sometimes, a time budget may be presented as a pie chart showing the duration of different behaviours observed by an animal over a set period.

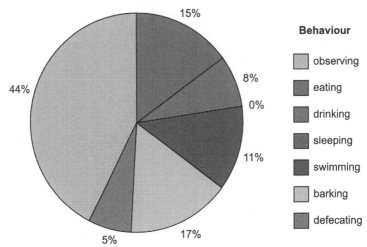

Time budget for an Australian sea lion over a 30 minute period

Alternatively, a table or chart showing how frequently certain behaviours are observed or how long they last can also be produced. Additionally, how long an animal takes to respond to a certain stimulus may be important, and therefore included in a chart. Ethograms and time budgets are very much specific to the aims of the study and the animals being observed.

Measuring and recording animal behaviour: Question

Go online

Q6: A student who was observing the behaviour of a lioness with one of her offspring made some field notes. Which of the following notes demonstrate anthropomorphism?

A) Offspring displayed teeth to mother.

B) Offspring begged mother for food.

C) Offspring pounced at mother.

D) Offspring smiled at mother.

. . . .

1.6 Learning points

Summary

- Often there are a wider range of hazards associated with fieldwork than laboratory work.

- Hazards, such as those resulting from uneven/challenging terrain, weather conditions and isolation, should be identified and the risks assessed.

- When sampling wild organisms, the technique chosen should be appropriate to the species being sampled.

- Techniques for sampling wild organisms include transects, point counts, remote detection, quadrats, camera traps and scat sampling.

- Sampling should be random, stratified and systematic.

- Organisms can be identified using keys, classification guides or analysis of DNA or proteins.

- Life can be classified into bacteria, archaea and eukaryotes.

- The plant kingdom has the major divisions: mosses, liverworts, ferns, gymnosperms and angiosperms.

- The animal kingdom is divided into phyla including: chordata, arthropoda, nematoda, platyhelminthes and mollusca.

- Monitoring populations is important in assessing environmental impact.

- Mark and recapture is a suitable technique for estimating population size: N = MC/R.

- Organisms can be marked using appropriate and effective techniques, including tagging, banding, surgical implantation, painting and hair clipping.

- Assumptions are made when carrying out mark and recapture studies.

- Ethograms and time sampling are used to compare the behaviour of different individuals of a species.

- In observing and recording animal behaviour anthropomorphism must be avoided.

1.7   End of topic test

End of Topic 1 test

Go online

Q7: State *two* additional risks or hazards associated with fieldwork compared to laboratory work. *(2 marks)*

....

Q8: Elusive species are difficult to sample. Name one technique used for sampling elusive species. *(1 mark)*

....

Q9: Which of the following statements correctly describes an example of stratified sampling? *(1 mark)*

a) A quadrat is placed every 2 m along a 20 m transect line.
b) 50 ladybirds are randomly chosen from a population of 500 ladybirds and their metabolic rate is measured.
c) 10 pupils from each year group in a school are randomly selected and their pulse rate is taken.

....

Q10: Identify which of the following correctly defines each taxonomic group. *(1 mark)*

a) Nematode: Parasitic flatworm; Angiosperm: Flowerless plant
b) Nematode: Parasitic roundworm; Angiosperm: Flowering plant
c) Nematode: Parasitic roundworm; Angiosperm: Flowerless plant
d) Nematode: Parasitic flatworm; Angiosperm: Flowering plant

....

Q11: Mark and recapture is a method used in monitoring populations. Give *two* methods for marking wild organisms. *(2 marks)*

....

Q12: The formula

$$N = \frac{MC}{R}$$

is used to estimate population size using mark and recapture data where:

- N = population estimate;
- M = number first captured, marked and released;
- C = total number in second capture;
- R = number marked in second capture.

In a survey to estimate a peppered moth population in Prince's Street Gardens, the following data were obtained.

- Number of peppered moths first captured, marked and released = 200
- Number of marked peppered moths in second capture = 70
- Number of unmarked peppered moths in second capture = 105

Calculate the estimated population of peppered moths in Prince's Street Gardens. *(1 mark)*

....

Q13: What is the study of animal behaviour called? *(1 mark)*

....

Q14: What are observations of animal behaviour recorded on? *(1 mark)*

....

Q15: What term is used to describe the personification of animal behaviour? *(1 mark)*

a) Anthropomorphism
b) Endomorphism
c) Homeomorphism
d) Pseudomorphism

....

....

Topic 2

Evolution

Contents

Prerequisite knowledge

You should already know that:

- *mutations are rare, random changes to genetic sequences which can be harmful, beneficial or neutral;*

- *genetic material can be passed horizontally in prokaryotes (bacteria);*

- *natural selection is a non-random process, resulting in a change to the frequency of certain genes occurring within a population;*

- *genetic drift is a random process, having greater effect on smaller populations, resulting in a change to the frequency of certain genes occurring within a population;*

- *symbiosis is the relationship between two organisms, each of a different species, whereby at least one of the two benefits.*

Learning objectives

By the end of this topic, you should be able to:

- *describe and explain the process of evolution with reference to sexual selection, natural selection and genetic drift;*

- *state that mutations give rise to genetic variation;*

- *define the terms absolute fitness and relative fitness;*

- *state that the rate of evolution can be increased by a number of factors and provide examples of such factors;*

- *explain, using examples, co-evolution and the Red Queen hypothesis.*

2.1   Drift and selection

Evolution is the change, over successive generations, in the proportion of individuals in a population differing in one or more inherited traits. Evolution can occur through the random process of **genetic drift** or the non-random processes of **natural selection** and **sexual selection**.

Genetic drift is the random change in how frequently a particular allele occurs within a population. Genetic drift has a more significant impact in small populations because alleles are more likely to be lost from the gene pool.

In the small population of just 17 individuals illustrated below, if some random chance event killed 8 individuals including all 4 blue individuals, the population would become uniformly red. This is an example of genetic drift.

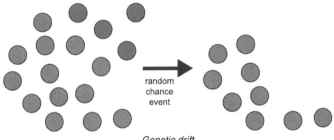

Genetic drift

In comparison to genetic drift, natural and sexual selection are non-random processes whereby certain alleles occur more frequently within a population because they confer a selective advantage. These alleles increase the chance that the individuals can compete and survive to pass the advantageous allele on to future generations.

The main source of novel alleles arising within a population is as a result of random **mutation**. Where the majority of mutations are deleterious or neutral, in very rare cases they may be beneficial to the fitness of an individual.

Fitness can be measured in absolute or relative terms.

- **Absolute fitness** is the ratio of frequencies of a particular genotype from one generation to the next. That is the ratio between the number of individuals with a particular genotype after selection, compared to the number with that same particular genotype before selection. If the absolute fitness is 1, then the frequency of that genotype is stable. A value greater than 1 conveys an increase in the genotype and, therefore, a value less than 1 conveys a decrease.

- **Relative fitness** is the ratio of surviving offspring of one genotype compared with other genotypes. For example, on average, pea plants with purple flowers produce more offspring than those with white flowers. Purple pea plants, as the most reproductively successful strain, are given a relative fitness of 1. If the white flowering pea plants only produce 65% as many offspring, their relative fitness would be 0.65 by comparison. As a result, the purple pea is the favoured trait and this allele would become more frequent in subsequent generations.

Drift and selection: Questions

Decide whether the following four attributes belong to genetic drift or natural/sexual selection.

Go online

Q1: Affects smaller populations.

a) Genetic drift
b) Natural or sexual selection

....

Q2: Alleles that give a selective advantage increase in frequency.

a) Genetic drift
b) Natural or sexual selection

....

Q3: Non-random.

a) Genetic drift
b) Natural or sexual selection

....

Q4: Random.

a) Genetic drift
b) Natural or sexual selection

....

Q5: The ratio of frequencies of a particular genotype from one generation to the next is defined as _____ fitness.

....

Q6: The ratio of surviving offspring of one genotype compared with other genotypes is defined as _____ fitness.

....

2.2   Rate of evolution

Where selection pressures are high, the rate of **evolution** can be rapid. The rate of evolution can be increased by factors such as:

- shorter generation times, which is why evolution tends to be so much more rapid in bacteria;

- warmer environments;

- sharing beneficial DNA sequences between different lineages through vertical gene transfer (sexual reproduction) and horizontal gene transfer.

The following diagram depicts the evolution of primates to humans, which has taken millions of years. This is due to the longer generation time.

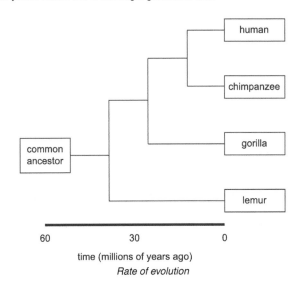

time (millions of years ago)
Rate of evolution

In comparison, evolution in bacteria is much quicker due to shorter generation times. The table below shows key dates involving the bacteria *Staphylococcus aureus*.

Year	Event
1880	Sir Alexander Ogston discovers *Staphylococcus aureus*.
1928	Sir Alexander Fleming discovers penicillin.
1943	Mass production of penicillin begins.
1945	Some *Staphylococcus aureus* show resistance to penicillin (PRSA).
1958	Antibiotic methicillin now used in treating penicillin resistant *Staphylococcus aureus*.
1961	Methicillin resistant *Staphylococcus aureus* emerge.
1966	Antibiotic vancomycin now used in treating methicillin resistant *Staphylococcus aureus*.
2001	Vancomycin resistant *Staphylococcus aureus* emerge.

Key dates involving the bacteria Staphylococcus aureus

As can be seen in the table above, *Staphylococcus aureus* has evolved resistance to three different antibiotics in just 60 years. This is due to the short generation time exhibited by bacteria.

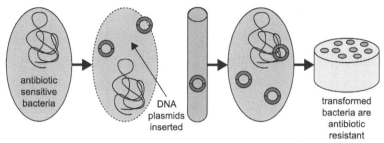

Horizontal gene transfer

Furthermore, as can be seen in the illustration above, bacteria can also transfer genes horizontally. In the example here, it is clear that the blue-coloured bacterium has a gene to give it resistance to an antibiotic. The resistant bacterium passes a copy of the gene to the sensitive (purple) bacteria, conferring it the same resistance. As a result of this process, favourable genes can be passed throughout populations and communities rapidly.

Rate of evolution: Questions

Q7: The following statements refer to factors which may or may not increase evolutionary rates.

Go online

1. Warmer environments.
2. Horizontal gene transfer.
3. Longer generation times.

Which statements would result in faster rates of evolution?

a) 1 only
b) 2 only
c) 3 only
d) 1 and 2
e) 1 and 3
f) 2 and 3
g) 1, 2 and 3

....

A new antibiotic has been developed against *Staphylococcus aureus*. The antibiotic is very effective. A *Staphylococcus aureus* outbreak occurs in a hospital and the new antibiotic is used.

Q8: Predict what will happen to the numbers of *Staphylococcus aureus* in the first year?

a) Numbers decrease
b) Numbers increase
c) Numbers stay the same

. . . .

Q9: Predict what will happen to the effectiveness of this new antibiotic over the next five years, justifying your answer.

. . . .

. . . .

2.3   Co-evolution and the Red Queen

Co-evolution is frequently seen in pairs of species that demonstrate a symbiotic relationship. Examples include:

- herbivores and plants;

- **pollinators** and plants;

- predators and their prey;

- **parasites** and their hosts.

Herbivores and plants

Plant grazers include herbivores, from insects and molluscs to large mammals. Plants have evolved both chemical and structural defences in response to grazing, including the production of deadly internal chemicals and toxins or external thorns and stings. Over many generations, grazers have subsequently undergone random mutations that have been favoured by **natural selection**, evolving to overcome some of these defences and so the race continues.   An example of co-evolution is the old world swallowtail caterpillar, living and feeding on the fringed rue plant. The rue produces toxic oils which deter plant-eating insects. The old world swallowtail caterpillar has evolved tolerance to these toxins, which allows it to continue to feed on the rue and has the added benefit of reducing competition with other plant-eating insects.

Caterpillar

Rue plant (Ruta graveolens)

In another example, seeds of the tropical leguminous grains, such as cowpeas and chickpeas, produce an amino acid which confers toxicity toward insects by inhibiting production of tRNA, reducing their ability to carry out protein synthesis. However, the bruchid beetle has evolved the ability to synthesise tRNA despite the presence of this toxic amino acid. This means that it can continue to utilise these seeds as a food source.

Pollinators and plants

The **symbiosis** between plants and their **pollinators** is an example of **mutualism**, whereby both species benefit. The white orchid, shown below, and African moths have co-evolved, with the moths receiving nutritious nectar and the flowers relying on the moths to spread pollen so they can reproduce.

White orchid

African moth

Flowers that are pollinated by birds produce nectar, which provides energy for the birds. To attract the birds, these flowers have undergone random mutations, favoured by natural selection to evolve their colour and shape to be best suited to attracting the pollinator in question. The following image shows the hummingbird pollinator. The flowering times of the plants on which it feeds are concurrent with the hummingbirds' breeding season, which is when the birds are more active and so more likely to require more nectar for energy.

Hummingbird pollinator

Furthermore, a mutualistic symbiotic relationship exists between the yucca plant and its pollinator, a species of yucca moth. The female moth pollinates the flowers of the yucca plant in return for a place to lay its eggs, deep within the flower where they are protected from any potential predators. The female moth leaves a chemical pheromone on the flower to alert other moths that this flower has been pollinated and that she has laid her eggs, thus ensuring that other moths lay their eggs in different flowers. When the eggs hatch, weeks later, the yucca has produced its fruit. The larvae feed on the seeds from this fruit. Neither the yucca plant nor the yucca moth would thrive without the other.

Predators and their prey

Predator-prey relationships are those involving predation, in which a predator eats its prey. Successful predators may have evolved adaptations, such as acute senses, claws, teeth, fangs, stingers or poison, that can help them to catch and feed on prey. Prey species have also evolved adaptations, from passive defences, such as hiding and camouflage, to active defenses, such as escaping or defending themselves. Poisonous arrow frogs in the Amazon rainforest are brightly coloured as a warning about the toxins that they produce in chemical defence against predators. A number of prey species have evolved mimicry, e.g. a harmless hornet looking like the vicious wasp.

Poison arrow frog

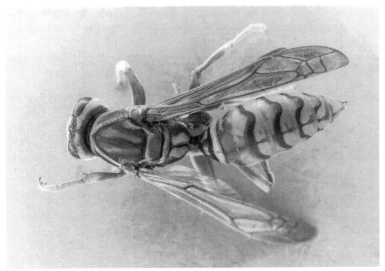

Harmless hornet

An example of co-evolution of predator and prey species is shown by rough-skinned newts and their predator, the common garter snake. The newts produce a deadly toxin that builds up in their skin. Garter snakes have evolved resistance to this, allowing them to prey upon the newts again. In response, newts have evolved again to further increase the toxicity of their skin. It would be predicted that co-evolution would continue, with each species evolving in response to the other.

Garter snake

Rough-skinned newt

Parasites and their hosts

Parasitism involves a relationship whereby a **parasite** lives on a host, gaining resources and a place to live. This is of benefit to the parasite, while the host is harmed. Co-evolution has been documented between the parasite that causes malaria, the mosquito that acts as a vector for this parasite and humans, which are the host. Current fossil evidence suggests that the parasite started to spread extensively about 100,000 years ago. This coincides with evidence to suggest when the first major human migrations took place. More recently, about 10,000 years ago, DNA sequence evidence suggests that both the parasite and mosquitoes underwent rapid evolution. Both of these events provide strong evidence for the complicated co-evolution between the parasite and the two other species; humans and mosquitoes.

Malaria mosquito

In co-evolution, a change in the traits of one species acts as a selection pressure on the other species, driving natural selection accordingly. The co-evolutionary 'arms race' between a parasite and host is known as the
Red Queen hypothesis *because both organisms must 'keep running in order to stay still'.*

The Red Queen analogy comes from the Alice in Wonderland story "Through the Looking Glass". In this story, Alice is seeking out the Queen of Hearts. The faster Alice runs to try and reach the Queen, the faster the Queen seems to go until, eventually, she vanishes. Alice is advised to go back the way she came and bumps right into the Queen. Alice is then lead by the Queen to the top of hill. Again the Queen runs. Alice starts running fast too, but when she and the Queen stop, neither has actually moved. Co-evolution is just like this, where evolution merely permits organisms to maintain their current success.

Co-evolution and the Red Queen: Questions

The following table compares slug parasitism by nematodes of two different slug populations.

Go online

- Slug population 1 - no previous exposure to nematode parasites.

- Slug population 2 - previous exposure to nematode parasites.

Time (weeks)	Number of nematodes in slug population 1	Number of nematodes in slug population 2
0	10	10
10	200	20
20	425	15
30	450	25
40	450	20

Q10: Calculate the percentage change in nematode numbers in slug population 1 from 10 to 20 weeks.

....

Q11: What evidence from the table suggests that slug population 2 has developed resistance to the nematodes?

....

Q12: How would this resistance have evolved?

....

Q13: In terms of the Red Queen hypothesis, predict what would happen to the numbers of nematode parasites in slug population 2 if left for a few generations.

....

2.4 Learning points

Summary

- Evolution is the change, over successive generations, in the proportion of individuals in a population differing in one or more inherited characteristics.

- Genetic drift is the random change in the frequency of a particular allele within a small population.

- Natural and sexual selection are non-random processes whereby certain alleles become more frequent within a population because they confer a selective advantage.

- The main source of novel alleles arising within a population is as a result of random mutations, most of which are deleterious or neutral, and, in very rare cases, may be beneficial to the fitness of an individual.

- Absolute fitness is the ratio of frequencies of a particular genotype from one generation to the next.

- Relative fitness is the ratio of surviving offspring of one genotype compared with other genotypes.

- Where selection pressures are high, the rate of evolution can be rapid.

- The rate of evolution can be increased by factors such as shorter generation times, warmer environments and the sharing of beneficial DNA sequences.

- In particular, sharing DNA sequences via horizontal gene transfer can result in very rapid evolution.

- Co-evolution will occur in pairs of species that interact with one another on a regular basis.

- Examples of co-evolution are found between herbivores and plants, pollinators and plants, predators and their prey, and parasites and their hosts.

- The co-evolutionary 'arms race' between a parasite and host is known as the Red Queen hypothesis, whereby a change in the traits of one species acts as a selection pressure on the other species.

2.5 End of topic test

End of Topic 2 test

Q14: Which random process that contributes to evolution affects smaller populations much more than larger populations? *(1 mark)*

Go online

....

Q15: What is the main source of new DNA sequences within a population? *(1 mark)*

....

Q16: When comparing the number of red genotypes to blue genotypes occurring within a butterfly population, what type of fitness is being measured? *(1 mark)*

....

Q17: Which 3 factors would collectively result in the greatest rate of evolution? *(1 mark)*

Cold environment	Longer generation time	Horizontal gene transfer
Warm environment	Shorter generation time	Vertical gene transfer

....

Q18: Explain why evolution is much more rapid in bacterial species when compared to primate species. *(2 marks)*

....

Q19: Which of the following co-evolved with parasites? *(1 mark)*

a) Herbivores
b) Hosts
c) Plants

....

Q20: Which of the following co-evolved with plants? *(1 mark)*

a) Herbivores
b) Hosts
c) Prey

....

Q21: Which of the following co-evolved with pollinators? *(1 mark)*

a) Herbivores
b) Plants
c) Prey

....

Q22: Which of the following co-evolved with predators? *(1 mark)*

a) Hosts
b) Plants
c) Prey

....

. . . .

Q23: What name is given to the hypothesis used to describe the continuous co-evolution of parasites and their hosts? *(1 mark)*

. . . .

Topic 3

Variation and sexual reproduction

Contents

Prerequisite knowledge

You should already know that:

- *sexual reproduction involves fusion of gametes from two different parents, resulting in dissimilar offspring, whereas asexual reproduction involves making exact copies of one parent;*

- *it is advantageous to have genetically varied offspring so that some may survive should conditions change;*

- *diploid refers to a cell with two full sets of chromosomes and haploid refers to a cell with just one full set of chromosomes;*

- *nuclear division is referred to as mitosis and results in all of the daughter cells being genetically identical to the mother cell;*

- *carriers are individuals who have a recessive allele that is masked by a dominant allele, yet they can pass this gene on to offspring;*

- *sex chromosomes (XY) determine the sex of an individual in many insect and mammal species.*

Learning objectives

By the end of this topic, you should be able to:

- *state the disadvantages of sexual reproduction;*
- *explain why, despite the disadvantages, sexual reproduction is so common;*
- *name successful asexual reproduction strategies;*
- *describe the stages of meiosis;*
- *describe the features of homologous chromosomes;*
- *state that meiosis results in variable gametes and describe the contribution of independent assortment and crossing over to this variation;*
- *define the term linked genes and explain how they are used to map chromosomes;*
- *state that environmental factors, for example temperature and resource availability, can affect sex ratio;*
- *define the term hermaphrodite;*
- *explain that the sex of some organisms can change due to competition or parasitic infection;*
- *explain why males are more likely to be affected by sex-linked conditions than females;*
- *explain that the random deactivation of genes on one of the X chromosomes in each cell prevents carrier females being affected by sex-linked genetic conditions.*

3.1 Costs and benefits of sexual and asexual reproduction

Compared to asexual reproduction, sexual reproduction appears to have two disadvantages.

1. Half of the population (males) are unable to produce offspring.

2. Each parent is only able to pass on half of their genetic material rather than the full 100%.

The benefits to sexual reproduction must, however, be greater than the disadvantages because it is so common. The benefits lie in the greater genetic variation within sexually reproducing organisms. This genetic variation provides some organisms with the ability to adapt to changing conditions or survive new strains of diseases. Without such genetic variety, the Red Queen's arms race (see Topic 2: "Evolution") would stop. In other words, this variation can drive selection and evolution should the different genes and alleles provide the individual with an advantage and, therefore, an increased chance of survival.

Where niches are narrow and stable, asexual reproduction can be a successful reproductive strategy. Asexual reproduction is also advantageous when recolonising disturbed habitats because it is usually faster. In eukaryotes, examples of asexual reproduction include:

- **vegetative propagation/cloning** in plants, such as reproduction via bulbs, e.g. onions and daffodils, and runners, e.g. spider plants and strawberry plants - all of the resulting offspring will be genetically identical to the original parent plant;

Daffodil bulbs   Flowering daffodils

Strawberry plant

Strawberry plant with runners by https://www.flickr.com/photos/gabrielahpaulin/, licenced under the Creative Commons https://creativecommons.org/licenses/by/2 .0/deed.en license

- **parthenogenic** animals lack fertilisation - embryos result from unfertilised eggs and, therefore, the resulting offspring will be haploid. When kept in captivity for several years with no male contact, female Komodo dragons have been known to reproduce without fertilisation. It appears that, for continuation of the species, this is how the female responds to isolation. This would be advantageous should females become isolated in the wild or should males die. The offspring of parthenogenesis in Komodo dragons are always male. Conversely, stick insects can also reproduce asexually in the absence of males; however, all of the offspring are female in this case. Parthenogenesis is found to be more common in cooler climates with low parasite diversity.

Komodo dragon

Stick insect

In organisms where asexual reproduction is most common, e.g. bacteria and yeast, many have mechanisms for horizontal gene transfer between individuals. This means that one individual can pass genetic information to another within the population, often via a connecting tube. Bacteria commonly pass plasmids between one another.

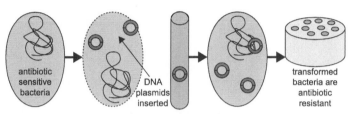

antibiotic sensitive bacteria — DNA plasmids inserted — transformed bacteria are antibiotic resistant

Horizontal gene transfer

Costs and benefits of reproduction: Questions

Go online

Q1: In fire ants, males may be produced by parthenogenesis from an egg cell. The diploid number of chromosomes is 8. When parthenogenesis occurs, how many chromosomes does a male fire ant have?

a) 2
b) 3
c) 4
d) 8

. . . .

Q2: Which term would be defined as "asexual reproduction in plants such as bulbs or runners"?

a) Horizontal gene transfer
b) Parthenogenesis
c) Vegetative propagation

. . . .

Q3: Which term would be defined as "asexual reproduction in reptiles where offspring are produced in the absence of fertilisation"?

a) Horizontal gene transfer
b) Parthenogenesis
c) Vegetative propagation

. . . .

Q4: Which term would be defined as "common in prokaryotes where sections of DNA, often in the form of plasmids, are passed between one another"?

a) Horizontal gene transfer
b) Parthenogenesis
c) Vegetative propagation

. . . .

3.2 Meiosis forms variable gametes

Meiosis is the process where gametes are produced in the reproductive organs. In animals, this takes place in the ovaries and testes. In plants, this takes place in the anthers and ovaries. One diploid gamete mother cell divides into four haploid sex cells.

Meiosis has two divisions and results in variable gametes. Division one is called meiosis I and division two is called meiosis II.

Meiosis I

1. Division 1 (meiosis I) starts with **interphase**. This is where each chromosome undergoes DNA replication to become two identical chromatids.

2. The **homologous chromosomes** pair up and line up along the equator of the cell.

3. Homologous chromosomes are pairs of chromosomes:

   - of the same size;
   - with the same centromere position;
   - with the same genes at the same loci.

4. The alleles of the genes on homologous chromosomes may, however, be dissimilar because each homologous chromosome is inherited from a different parent.

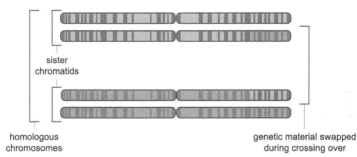

sister chromatids

homologous chromosomes

genetic material swapped during crossing over

Homologous chromosomes

5. When the homologous chromosomes pair up, they can touch each other at points called **chiasmata**. **Crossing over** can then occur at chiasmata. This is when sections of DNA get swapped, shuffling sections of DNA between the homologous pairs, allowing the recombination (creation of new combinations) of alleles to occur.

6. Another process in meiosis I that results in variation between gametes is **independent assortment**. When homologous chromosomes pair up and line up along the equator, the final position of one pair is completely random relative to every other pair. Additionally, these chromosomes go on to be separated, irrespective of their maternal and paternal origin. This means that independent assortment results in gametes with varying combinations of maternal and paternal chromosomes.

7. The number of possible combinations is worked out by calculating 2 (since there are two of each chromosome inherited - one from each parent) to the power of however many chromosome pairs there are. In humans, there are 23 pairs of chromosomes, thus the haploid number is 23. Therefore, the number of possible combinations in the gamete is:

$$2^{23} = 8,388,608 \ combinations$$

8. Homologous chromosomes are separated by spindle fibres and are pulled to opposite ends of the cell.

9. The cell divides, forming two haploid daughter cells.

Meiosis II

1. In division 2 (meiosis II), chromatids are separated by spindle fibres and four haploid gametes (often genetically dissimilar) are formed.

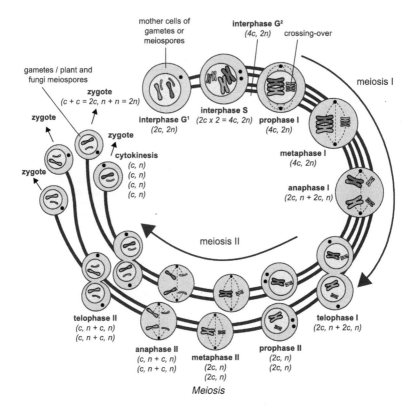

Meiosis

In many organisms, gametes (sex cells) are formed directly from the cells that are produced by meiosis. In other groups, mitosis may follow meiosis to form a haploid organism. Gametes form later from this haploid organism or by cellular differentiation. This is unlikely to occur in animals; however, it has been observed in some types of fungi and in plants such as algae. Green algae are a good example, the life cycle of which alternates between two types of reproductive cycles. In the first cycle, algal cells exist as haploid cells which then fuse with other haploid algal cells, forming diploid zygotes. In the second cycle, the diploid individuals that were formed during the first cycle carry out meiosis, producing haploid zoospores. These zoospores remain haploid and the first cycle begins again.

Linked genes and chromosome mapping

Genes on the same chromosome are said to be linked. Genes that are situated closely on a chromosome are less likely to be separated during crossing over, whereas genes that are further apart are much more likely to be separated. Separating **linked genes** through crossing over creates **recombinants**. Scientists use the frequency of recombination to map chromosomes, working out where each gene is in relation to others and pinpointing exact locations on the chromosome. An example of how recombination frequency is used to map chromosomes is given below.

In certain organisms, genes A, B, C and D are located on the same chromosome. The percentage recombination between pairs of these genes is shown in the following table.

Gene pair	Percentage recombination
A and B	15
A and C	5
B and D	5
C and D	25

Since genes C and D have a percentage recombination of 25%, they will be quite far apart on the chromosome. Conversely, with a percentage recombination of just 5%, genes A and C will be closer to one another. The best thing to do is to draw a straight line to represent your chromosome, then start to write letters in, making sure that the numbers work. This can take a little trial and error so use a pencil.

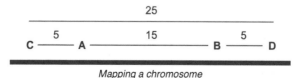

Mapping a chromosome

Go online

Meiosis forms variable gametes: Activity

Q5:   Arrange the following key steps in the process of meiosis in the correct order.

- Chromatids are separated by spindle fibres.
- Chromosomes undergo DNA replication (interphase).
- Crossing over occurs at points called chiasmata.
- Four haploid gametes are produced.
- Homologous chromosomes line up at the equator of the cell.
- Homologous chromosomes touch at points called chiasmata.
- Independent assortment occurs.
- Two haploid cells are formed.

....

Meiosis forms variable gametes: Questions

Go online

A mosquito has six chromosomes.

Q6:   What is its diploid number?

....

Q7:   What is its haploid number?

....

Q8:   How many different combinations are possible in the gametes of a mosquito?

....

Q9:   In *Drosophila*, the genes for wing length (L), eye colour (C), body colour (B) and the presence of bristles (P) are linked (all on the same chromosome). The following table gives the frequency of recombination obtained in crosses involving different pairs of linked genes.

Gene pair in the cross	Frequency of recombination (%)
Wing length x Eye colour	12
Wing length x Body colour	18
Wing length x Presence of bristles	16
Eye colour x Presence of bristles	4
Body colour x Presence of bristles	2

Use the information to show the positions of these genes in relation to each other on a chromosome diagram. Work out in which order the linked genes L, C, B and P would appear on the chromosome.

....

3.3   Sex determination

Many organisms, usually invertebrates, are **hermaphroditic**.   Simultaneous
hermaphrodites are organisms with both male and female reproductive organs, e.g.
earthworms and slugs. Sequential hermaphrodites are born as one sex and may change
to the other sex at some point during their life, e.g. some fish and jellyfish. This usually
happens if reproductive success is likely to be much greater by being the other sex.

Sometimes, sex determination is under environmental rather that genetic control.
Crocodiles and alligators are a good example of this.   In Nile crocodiles, if the
temperature inside the nest, and therefore the egg incubation temperature, is below
31.7°C or above 34.5°C, the offspring will be female. Males are only born in the narrow
range between these two temperatures.

Nile crocodile

In some species, the sex ratio of offspring can be adjusted in response to population
density and the resulting strain on resource availability. This has been observed in deer.
There has been a correlation between dominant females producing greater numbers
of male offspring. How this manipulation occurs is yet to be explained, however, the
female seems to be able to control sex selection. Some theories suggest that the
female can detect the differently shaped sperm responsible for sex determination and
can control them as they move through the reproductive tract. During times of higher
population density and excessive winter rainfall, this relationship between dominant
females producing more males was no longer found. This finding has been linked to
poorer nutrition in pregnant females.

Changing sex

Some species of animals have been found to change their sex during their lifetime. Sex can change as a result of size, competition or parasitic infection. However, the underlying reason for a change in sex will be to permit the occurrence of successful reproduction. Male shrimps have been found to change into females in response to parasitic infection. In anemone fish, all juveniles are males. On forming monogamous pairs, one of the fish will become female. Should the female die, the male in the pair becomes female and a new juvenile male moves into the pair. In another type of fish, the bluebanded goby, when a dominant male dies, a large female will take his place, changing gender to do so. The female starts to display more aggressive behaviour and undergoes changes in hormone levels.

Sex chromosomes and sex linkage

In mammals, and some insects such as *Drosophila* and butterflies, sex is determined through a set of specific chromosomes - the sex chromosomes. Usually, these are known as the X and Y chromosomes, with a gene on the Y chromosome often determining the development of 'maleness'.

Males are said to be **heterogametic** because their sex chromosomes are dissimilar (XY). The male lacks homologous alleles on the smaller (Y) chromosome. This can result in sex-linked patterns of inheritance whereby males have a greater chance of being affected by certain recessive conditions, e.g. colour blindness and haemophilia in humans. This is because females would need two copies of the recessive allele to be affected, whereas males only need one.

Females may be carriers, thus have one copy of the affected gene, yet remain unaffected. They can, however, pass this onto any offspring they have. In females, the parts of the X chromosome that are absent from the Y chromosome are randomly inactivated in one of the homologous X chromosomes in each cell in the body. This prevents a double-dose of gene products. This also means that carriers will not suffer from the effects of any harmful mutations on these X chromosomes because the X chromosome inactivation is random and 50% of the cells in any tissue will have a normal copy of the gene in question.

A good example of a sex-linked gene in humans is haemophilia. This is a condition where the affected individual does not produce the blood clotting agent Factor VIII. Haemophilia is the result of a recessive gene carried on the X chromosome. If we use the letter "N" for normal and "n" for affected, we can produce the following genotypes:

- Normal male = $X^N Y$

- Affected male = $X^n Y$

- Normal female = $X^N X^N$

- Carrier female = $X^N X^n$

- Affected female = $X^n X^n$

In the following cross, a normal male is crossed with a carrier female.

Parents X^NY x X^NX^n

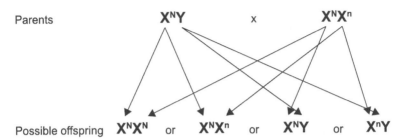

Possible offspring X^NX^N or X^NX^n or X^NY or X^nY

As can be seen here, a range of phenotypes may be expected, yet the only affected individual is a son. To be affected, the male only requires one recessive gene; however, the female needs two haemophilia genes to be affected. In the carrier female, the haemophilia gene is masked by the normal gene; however, she has a 50% chance of passing this gene to her offspring and any sons she passes it to will have haemophilia.

Tortoiseshell cat

In cats, a tortoiseshell coat results from a mixture of black and red. The red coat colour gene is dominant (O) to cream (o) and is carried on the X chromosome. Red is also dominant to black; however, black is dominant to cream. The black coat colour gene is not sex-linked, therefore it must be on an **autosome**. In males, which have only one X chromosome, if their X chromosome has a red coat colour gene, then they will have a red coat. In female carriers, X^OX^o will have a patchy coat, with red in places and black being able to show through in other places. This is due to the random inactivation of one of the two X chromosomes in every cell in the cat.

Go online

Sex determination: Questions

Eggs from Nile crocodiles were incubated at two different temperatures over five breeding seasons. When the crocodiles hatched, their sex was recorded. The following graph shows the affect that temperature had on gender within the population.

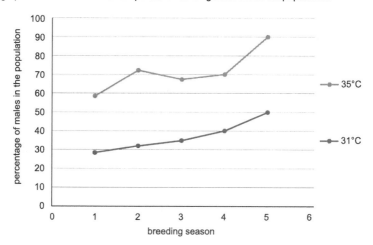

Q10: Calculate the percentage change in females in the population between breeding seasons 4 and 5 when incubated at 35 °C.

....

Q11: Calculate the percentage change in males in the population between breeding seasons 4 and 5 when incubated at 31 °C.

....

Q12: How many females would be present in a population of 400 Nile crocodiles after 4 breeding seasons at 31 °C?

....

Q13: How many males would be present in a population of 600 Nile crocodiles after 5 breeding seasons at 35 °C?

....

Q14: Haemophilia is a recessive sex linked condition carried on the X chromosome. In a cross between an affected male and a carrier female, what are the chances that any offspring will be affected?

....

Q15: In the same cross, what are the chances that a son will be affected?

....

Q16: In the same cross, what are the chances that a daughter will be affected?

....

3.4 Learning points

Summary

- There are two disadvantages of sexual reproduction. Only females can produce offspring and each parent only passes on 50% of their genes rather than the full 100%.

- The one advantage of sexual reproduction is the huge genetic variability amongst offspring, which outweighs any disadvantages.

- Asexual reproduction is ideal in stable niches and includes strategies in eukaryotes, such as vegetative propagation in plants and parthenogenesis in some insects and reptiles

- For prokaryotes, where reproduction tends to be asexual, horizontal gene transfer between individuals is a common mechanism.

- Meiosis is the process whereby one diploid gamete mother cell divides into four genetically dissimilar haploid gametes.

- Independent assortment and crossing over both occur in meiosis I and are responsible for increasing the genetic variation amongst gametes.

- Homologous chromosomes are pairs of chromosomes of the same size, with the same centromere position and with the same genes at the same loci.

- The alleles of the genes on homologous chromosomes may, however, be dissimilar because each homologous chromosome is inherited from a different parent.

- Linked genes are found on the same chromosome. The frequency of linked chromosomes being separated through crossing over can be used to map chromosomes.

- Hermaphrodites are organisms with both male and female reproductive organs.

- In some organisms, such as crocodiles, environmental conditions can affect the sex ratio of offspring.

- In other cases, the sex ratio is related to resource availability.

- Some organisms can change their sex in their lifetime depending on environmental conditions, parasitic infection or competition.

- In mammals, males tend to be heterogametic. This means that sex linked traits are more common in males than females.

- Females can be carriers of a recessive sex-linked trait, yet show no deleterious effects.

> **Summary continued**
>
> • The reason for this is that one X chromosome in each cell is randomly deactivated so that half of the cells will contain an active working copy of the gene.

3.5   Extended response question

The activity which follows presents an extended response question similar to the style that you will encounter in the examination.

You should have a good understanding of meiosis before attempting the question.

You should give your completed answer to your teacher or tutor for marking, or try to mark it yourself using the suggested marking scheme.

Extended response question: Meiosis

Give an account of meiosis. *(10 marks)*

....

3.6   End of topic test

Go online

End of Topic 3 test

Q17: Males being unable to produce offspring is one disadvantage of sexual reproduction. What is the other disadvantage of sexual reproduction that is universal to all species? *(1 mark)*

a) Finding a mate is difficult.
b) Not all individuals are attracted to the opposite sex.
c) Only half of each parent's genome is passed onto offspring.
d) Genetic variation decreases.

....

Q18: Sexual reproduction leads to genetic variation _____. *(1 mark)*

a) decreasing
b) increasing
c) staying the same

....

Q19: Which of the following statements about parthenogenesis is not true? *(1 mark)*

a) Unfertilised eggs develop into embryos.
b) This is common in plants.

c) Offspring are haploid.

d) It is common in cooler climates.

....

Q20: Which of the following statements are true of meiosis I only? *(1 mark)*

A) Crossing over occurs at points called chiasmata.

B) Independent assortment occurs.

C) Homologous chromosomes are separated.

D) Four haploid gametes are produced.

....

Q21: State two features of homologous chromosomes. *(2 marks)*

....

Q22: Name two processes that are responsible for increasing genetic variation during meiosis. *(2 marks)*

....

Q23: Genes on the same chromosome are said to be _____. *(1 mark)*

....

Q24: What term is used to describe an individual with both male and female reproductive organs? *(1 mark)*

....

Q25: Which of these terms means that the sex chromosomes are dissimilar? *(1 mark)*

a) Heterogametic

b) Hermaphroditic

c) Recombination

d) Sex-linked

....

Q26: In sex linked conditions in humans, the male requires _____ of the affected gene to show the condition in their phenotype. *(1 mark)*

a) one copy

b) two copies

....

Q27: In sex linked conditions in humans, the female requires _____ of the affected gene to show the condition in their phenotype. *(1 mark)*

a) one copy

b) two copies

....

Q28: Explain why carrier females remain unaffected by deleterious mutations carried on the X chromosome? *(1 mark)*

....

Topic 4

Sex and behaviour

Contents

Prerequisite knowledge

You should already know that:

- *sperm are smaller and produced in greater numbers than eggs;*

- *males often have to compete or display for females, who will then choose the fittest;*

- *parental care has a high energy demand; however, this technique increases the chance of reproductive success;*

- *sexual selection is a type of natural selection by which females choose males based on certain physical characteristics.*

Learning objectives

By the end of this topic, you should be able to:

- *compare sexual investment between males and females;*
- *explain the problems faced by sessile organisms in relation to sex, and describe solutions to these problems;*
- *state that parental investment is costly, but greatly increases the chance of successful reproduction;*
- *compare the features of r-selected and K-selected organisms;*
- *state that classification of parental investment into discrete r-selected or K-selected categories fails to reflect the complex range of life history strategies;*
- *explain the correlation between the reproductive strategy employed, and the number and quality of current offspring versus possible future offspring;*
- *define the term sexual dimorphism;*
- *describe male-male rivalry in courtship behaviour, explaining that smaller males may use a variety of techniques such as sneaking;*
- *explain that successful courtship behaviour in birds and fish can be a result of species-specific sign stimuli and fixed action pattern responses;*
- *define the term imprinting and discuss the effect it may have on mate choice later in life;*
- *explain that females use courtship behaviour to make choices based on male fitness, usually related to advantageous genes or low parasite infestation;*
- *using examples, explain what lekking is.*

4.1 Sexual investment

Sperm versus egg production

In animals, sperm are always far more numerous than eggs. Due to the presence of an energy store, eggs are much larger and fewer in number. A far greater investment is made by females due to the production of a lower number of larger gametes. As a result, their chance of reproductive success is lower and the chance of passing on genes is reduced.

Sessile organisms

Sessile organisms are those that are fixed to a surface and therefore cannot move. Plants are usually sessile. There are good examples from the animal kingdom though, such as barnacles and corals. Being sessile does pose some problems in terms of sex. How do individuals find a mate and how do gametes meet? In sessile animals, such as corals, stages within their lifecycle are mobile. This is particularly clear in the larval stage of corals. Clouds containing millions of gametes are released into the water simultaneously, thus increasing the chance of successful fertilisation. The larvae that result from fertilisation are motile for a period of time. Slow moving and sessile organisms are often hermaphroditic (see Topic 3) or employ parasitism as a reproductive strategy. Barnacles, for example, are hermaphroditic. They use extremely long sex organs to reach another for the transfer of sperm.

Barnacles living on mussels

Of course, reproduction does not have to be sexual and, if conditions are unsuitable for successful sexual reproduction, some organisms may revert to asexual reproduction. Success may be greater, although genetic variation will be lost (see Topic 3).

In plants, insects and wind have a vital role in successfully allowing pollination. Bees and other flying insects are extremely important for carrying pollen from one flower to the stigma of another. Flowers and pollinators are in very close symbiotic relationships (see Topic 2). Flower shape and structure is suited to its specific pollinator, enhancing the success of pollination and ultimately reproduction.

Costs and benefits of external and internal fertilisation

Internal fertilisation is the process by which the sperm and egg nuclei fuse inside the female. Conversely, external fertilisation is when this fusion occurs outside the female. In external fertilisation, large numbers of eggs and sperms are released into the water and fertilisation occurs in the absence of parents. External water is essential here to prevent gametes from drying out and to provide a medium for sperm to swim to eggs. External water is essential here to prevent drying of the gametes and to provide a medium for sperm to swim to eggs. Courtship behaviour is important in external fertilisation because timing is crucial to ensure that mature sperm and ripe eggs meet. Environmental stimuli, such as temperature or day length, may cause all the individuals of a population to release their gametes at the same time, while chemical signals from one individual releasing gametes may trigger gamete release in others.

Internal fertilisation is necessary where no external moisture is available. Cooperative behaviour which ultimately leads to copulation is required. Internal fertilisation requires highly advanced reproductive systems.

External fertilisation in frogs by http://www. flickr.com/people/63048706@N06, licenced under the Creative Commons http s://creativecommons.org/licenses/by/2.0/d eed.en license

This frog carries the tadpoles on her back until she finds water by http://flickr.com/pe ople/19731486@N07, licenced under the Creative Commons https://creativecommo ns.org/licenses/by/2.0/deed.en license

Protection and care

All species produce more offspring than survive to reproduce. Species with external fertilisation usually produce enormous numbers of gametes, but the proportion that are successfully fertilised, survive and develop further is often quite small. Internal fertilisation usually produces fewer offspring; however, success is usually greater. Embryos are offered greater protection and parental care is high. Types of protection that require a greater input of energy include:

- resistant eggshells;
- development of the embryo within the female parent;

- parental care of eggs and offspring.

Birds and reptiles produce eggs with calcium and protein shells that can withstand cold, dry, hot environments with rough terrain. In comparison, the eggs of fish and amphibians have only a gelatinous coat.

In mammals, embryos develop within the uterus, obtaining nourishment from the mother's blood supply via the placenta.

When a bird hatches or a mammal is born, it is still not capable of independent existence. Adult birds endure the demands of feeding their chicks and mammals nurse their offspring with milk produced by the mother. There are, however, endless examples of parental care, including some rather peculiar methods, all with the ultimate goal of increasing the chance of survival of the offspring. In one species of tropical frog, for example, the father carries the tadpoles inside his stomach until they hop out as frogs!

Parental investment

Parental investment is costly but increases the chance that young will survive. The level of parental care will depend on the number of offspring produced and the environment. In a stable environment, organisms tend to produce a smaller number of rather 'expensive' young, thus a lot of energy will be invested in caring for each one. Conversely, in unstable environments, many 'cheap' young are produced with low energy investment and parental care.

These particular life history strategies can be categorised into two groups:

1. **r-selected** populations;

2. **K-selected** populations.

Characteristic	r-selected population	K-selected population
Environment	Unstable	Stable
Maturation time	Short	Long
Lifespan	Short	Long
Death rate	Usually high	Usually low
Number of offspring produced per reproductive episode	Many	Few
Number of reproductions in lifetime	Usually one	Often several
Timing of first reproduction	Early in life	Later in life
Size of offspring or eggs	Small	Large
Parental care	None	Often extensive

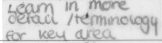
Learn in more detail /terminology for key area

It is difficult, though, to place organisms discretely into one of the two groups. There are many exceptions, and most sit somewhere along the scale between r-selected and K-selected. For example, trees can live for many years, in some cases hundreds, but produce massive numbers of offspring, thus displaying traits of both. Similarly, reptiles, such as sea turtles, display both r- and K-traits; although sea turtles are large in size, with very long life spans (provided they reach adulthood), they produce large numbers of offspring that receive no parental care. Furthermore, mammalian males tend to be r-type reproducers due to copious numbers of sperm, whereas females tend to have K-characteristics, producing far fewer eggs. There are many examples where organisms do not fit neatly into either category.

Life histories vary greatly from species to species. Pacific salmon spawn in small streams, then migrate to open ocean where they feed and grow for a number of years. Eventually, they journey back upstream to their spawning grounds, release huge numbers of gametes in a single reproductive event and then they die. There are clear characteristics here of r-selected species. In contrast, some lizards reproduce every year for a number of years and only lay a few large eggs.

The life histories of plants are just as variable. Some species of oaks do not reproduce until the 20th year, but then produce vast numbers of large seeds each year for over 100 years. Annual desert wildflowers generally germinate, grow, reproduce and die all within the period of a month after spring rains. Complicating matters further, important characteristics of life history may vary significantly among populations of a single species or even among individuals within the same population.

Optimal reproduction

Optimal reproduction is based on the premise of a trade-off in terms of the number and quality of current offspring versus potential future offspring. Some plants and animals, such as desert annual plants, many insects and Pacific salmon, invest most of their energy in maturation, expending this energy in one single reproductive event before dying. Other organisms produce fewer offspring at a time over a number of successive seasons. The relative advantage of each strategy can be thought of in terms of a trade-off between fertility and survival probability. If an organism is to breed over a number of successive seasons, it must invest some energy in survival mechanisms. Unfortunately, if the organism dies before reproducing again, these resources have been wasted. A general rule is that organisms with a low survival chance between reproductive events will have one reproductive event, whereas those that survive well once established will have more than one, smaller reproductive events. Organisms inhabiting unstable, unpredictable or harsh environments will likely have one large reproductive event.

Polygamy versus monogamy

In many species, mating is promiscuous, with short-lasting relationships. In species where bonds are formed, the relationship may be described as monogamous (one male mating with one female) or polygamous (an individual of one sex mating with several of the other). Polygamous relationships most commonly are between a single male and many females.

Most birds choose **monogamy** due to the high level of parental care needed in feeding the chicks. It is unlikely that one parent could meet these feeding and protecting requirements alone. In a monogamous relationship, male birds probably have a better chance of leaving more viable offspring by participating in parental care than searching for other mates. In mammals, the female is often the only food source for the young by means of the milk that she produces. Males may have a role in protection, but not feeding, therefore **polygamy** is common here with one male mating with many females in a harem, and protecting them and his offspring, as seen in deer and lions.

Another factor that influences reproductive strategy is certainty of paternity. The female who gives birth or lays the eggs is certain of maternity. However, even within a normally monogamous relationship, the male cannot be 100% sure of paternity.

A mammal with an insect's strategy

A particularly unusual reproductive strategy is employed by the naked mole-rat. Naked mole-rats are indigenous to the hot, dry areas of Kenya and Ethiopia. Like social insects, they live in underground colonies numbering between 100 and 300 individuals, and only a single 'queen' reproduces with one or two males. The rest of the colony assume the role of 'worker' or 'soldier'. Only 2% of the colony are fertile at any one time. Infertility of the others can be reversed if the queen dies. This reproductive strategy seems to have evolved in naked mole-rats due to the harsh conditions in which they live. Low rainfall, lack of food and hard ground means that living in social groups in shared burrows will increase survival in such an inhospitable environment. Due to genetic relatedness, the fitness of non-breeding individuals will be far greater within a colony than it would be with a solitary existence.

Naked mole-rat in its burrow

Go online

Sexual investment: Activity

Q1:   Complete the table using the attributes listed.

Characteristic	r-selected population	K-selected population
Environment		
Lifespan		
Number of offspring per reproductive episode		
Number of reproductions in lifetime		
Size of offspring or eggs		
Parental care		

Attributes: few, large, long, many, none, often extensive, often several, short, small, stable, unstable, usually one.

. . . .

4.2   Courtship

Sexual dimorphism

Sexual dimorphism is defined as any physical differences between males and females. It is often expressed as a difference in size with the male usually being larger, but it also involves such features as colourful plumage in male birds, manes on male lions, antlers on male deer and other adornments. In most cases of sexual dimorphism, the male is conspicuous and the female very inconspicuous. It makes sense for the female to be inconspicuous because she may carry and protect young, so an ability to camouflage or blend in will increase her and her offspring's chance of survival. In some cases, the male with the most impressive masculine features may be the most attractive to females. Secondary sex structures may also be larger, allowing males to compete with other males for females, e.g. antlers. These structures are often used for show, in an effort to appear threatening without the need for violence.

Darwin considered sexual dimorphism to be a product of sexual selection. This was because many of the features displayed in males, such as the plumage of peacocks, do not confer an advantage to survival in their environment, and in some cases can attract predators or merely get in the way. If these structures increase the individual's chance of gaining a mate, however, they will be favoured because they enhance reproductive success. In the case of male peacocks, a beautiful plumage will demonstrate fitness and imply a low parasite burden - attractive characteristics to a female.

Grand plumage of the peacock   *Male lion characterised by its mane*

In most species, females are very choosy; picking a poor-quality male can be a costly error. Males must therefore win at least one, but in most cases many females. In some animals, competition or rivalry among males almost entirely determines which animals will mate. In other species, females assess mates based on specific behaviours which she observes in the male, e.g. keeping a tidy, clean nest or foraging for sufficient quantities of food of a good quality. Such behaviours are important because they provide the female with an idea of how much parental care the male may offer. For example, male common terns (which are similar to gulls) carry fish and display them to potential mates as part of the mating ritual. Eventually, a male may begin to feed fish to a female. This behaviour conveys a male's ability to provide food for chicks. In other species, females choose males who exhibit extreme and energetic courtship displays or who have the most extreme secondary sex characteristics, such as a long tail. Perhaps these features indicate that the male is vigorous and in good health, thus a sign of fitness. Fitness can be defined in terms of good genes and low parasite burden.

Lekking

In a number of bird and insect species, males display communally in a small area called a **lek**. Females visit the lek and choose among displaying males by assessing whether signals are 'honest' and are really a sign of male fitness. They will look for good condition and low parasite density, both implied by a healthy plumage. A healthy plumage can be used to infer that the male has strong genes against parasites and diseases, clear traits that the female would want for her offspring

Black Grouse in a lek by http://www.flickr.com/people/41502344@N02, licenced under the Creative Commons https://creativecommons.org/licenses/by/2.0/deed.en license

After females makes their choice, mating occurs, after which there is no further contact between females and males.

Alternative mating strategies - sneaking behaviour in males

Sneaking behaviour refers to a strategy that allows smaller, less threatening males to more stealthily access a female partner, often avoiding altercations with dominant males. These sneaking males are often called **satellite males**.

Large horned beetles develop very large horns that they use as weapons for fighting for females. Smaller horned beetles do not possess such weaponry so adopt alternative mating strategies. Beetles with long horns will guard their mate by protecting the entrance to the tunnel. These males will fight any male that tries to enter. Smaller males with little or no horns have little chance of beating larger males so opt for a sneaking strategy. These satellite males dig a new tunnel that allows them access to the female's tunnel, unnoticed by the male guard. Since both of these strategies have proven, thus far, to be reproductively effective for the males that practice them, male horned beetles continue to have two very different, yet successful, phenotypes.

Rhinoceros beetle with large horn   *Bluegill sunfish*

Sneaking behaviour is also common in many fish species. Male Bluegill sunfish come in three different size morphs.

1. A large male that courts females, and then defends a nest in which he rears young.

2. A medium sized satellite or sneaker male that successfully fertilises eggs by mimicking the females in order to interrupt courtship between the female and a large male.

3. A very small satellite that dives in between a mating pair and squirts ejaculate in order to fertilise eggs.

All three mating types mentioned above are considered by researchers to have approximately equal fitness.

Species with larger females than males

In some species there may be reversed sexual dimorphism where the female is more conspicuous. This is common amongst insects, spiders, fish, reptiles and birds of prey. There are some cases in mammals, e.g. spotted hyenas and blue whales. Males are often smaller in species where they may have long distances to travel in search of females. Obviously, a smaller size will be an advantage for speed and stealth.

One example of sexual size dimorphism is the black myotis bat. Females are significantly larger than males in body weight, skull size and forearm length. Females are thought to be larger because they have the higher energetic costs of producing eggs in comparison to the 'cheaper' lower energetic costs faced by males in sperm production. Larger mothers are an advantage in organisms where gestation and lactation last for quite a number of months, such as the black myotis bat where females suckle their offspring until nearly adult size. They would not be able to continue flying and catching prey if they were not larger, thus able to support the additional mass of the offspring during this time.

Some species of angler fish display extreme reversed sexual dimorphism. Females are much larger than males. Males live almost a parasitic existence with an underdeveloped digestive system. Upon finding a mate, the male fuses with her, embarking upon a parasitic existence and becoming little more than a sperm-producing body.

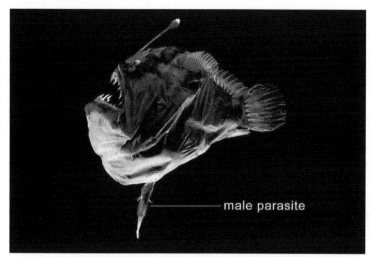

Female angler fish with the smaller male attached by Edith Widder / EOL, licenced under the Creative Commons https://creativecommons.org/licenses/by-nc-sa/3.0/ license / "male parasite" label added

There are many more examples of reversed sexual dimorphism in nature.

Species-specific signals

Animals often use signals that only other members of the same species understand. These may include giving off chemicals, or making sounds or certain displays to initiate mating. This means that individuals mate when most fertile, increasing the chance of successful reproduction. In birds and fish, in particular, successful courtship behaviour can be a result of species-specific sign stimuli and the resulting fixed action pattern responses. These signs and signals will be innate, thus instinctive.

A good example of fixed action patterns has been observed in male three-spine sticklebacks. During mating season, the male will develop a red colour on his throat. This sign stimulus attracts females and entices aggression in other males. The male builds a nest, attacking any males that try to enter, whilst courting and attracting females. Using stickleback models, researchers discovered that males respond aggressively to the red throat stimulus. Conversely, when a model with a swollen stomach was used, males responded by demonstrating courtship behaviour. These fixed action patterns will increase fitness by increasing the chance of successful mating.

Male three-spined stickleback with red throat by Piet Spaans, licenced under the Creative Commons https://creativecommons.org/licenses/by-nc-sa/3.0/ license

Imprinting

Imprinting is an irreversible, rapid developmental process that occurs during a critical time period in young birds where the young bird fixates on a larger object (hopefully this is the parent and not a predator). Recent studies show that imprinting, and what is learned during this time with regards to social behaviour and sexual selection, may influence mate choice later in life.

Courtship: Questions

Go online

Q2: The difference in phenotypic appearance between males and females of a species is a definition of:

a) imprinting.
b) lekking.
c) sexual dimorphism.
d) sneaking behaviour.

. . . .

Q3: The process by which male birds display in a communal area so that females can assess and choose a mate is a definition of:

a) imprinting.
b) lekking.
c) sexual dimorphism.
d) sneaking behaviour.

....

Q4: A smaller male that gains access to females without other dominant males knowing is a definition of:

a) imprinting.
b) lekking.
c) sexual dimorphism.
d) sneaking behaviour.

....

Q5: An irreversible process in young birds at a critical time where they fixate on a larger object is a definition of:

a) imprinting.
b) lekking.
c) sexual dimorphism.
d) sneaking behaviour.

....

The table below shows how parasite infestation affects mating success in male capercaillies. Mating success is measured as how many times a male is selected by a female to mate during the breeding season.

Parasite abundance	Average number of times the male is selected by a female
Low	35 +/- 1.5
Medium	15 +/- 1.5
High	2 +/- 1.5

Q6: Present the information in the table as a bar graph.

....

Q7: Calculate the percentage change in the number of times a male is selected when parasitism rises from low to medium.

....

Q8: What conclusion can be drawn about parasite abundance and mating success?

....

Q9: Suggest why parasite abundance is a useful way for females to assess males.

....

....

4.3 Learning points

Summary

- Egg production, with their energy store and larger size, involves a far greater energy investment than sperm production, meaning that females have a greater sexual investment.

- Sessile organisms use asexual reproduction, hermaphroditism, mass release of gametes and very long penises, as appropriate, to increase their reproductive success.

- Organisms will employ the most successful reproductive strategy possible, assessing the number and quality of current offspring against the potential for future offspring.

- Organisms can be classed as r-selected or K-selected organisms based on their reproductive strategy and life history, although organisms can display traits of both groups.

- Sexual dimorphism is when males and females of the same species have very different physical appearance, often in terms of colour and size - this is a result of sexual selection.

- Females are usually inconspicuous.

- Sexual dimorphism can be reversed in some species.

- Male-male rivalry sees larger males, often with appendages used a weapons, having greater success at finding a mate.

- Smaller males may employ sneaking behaviour and see equal success at gaining access to females.

- Successful courtship is often the result of species-specific sign stimuli that bring about a fixed action pattern response.

- Imprinting is an irreversible process in young birds where they fixate on a larger living thing for protection and nurturing; this may affect mate choice later in life.

- Lekking is when males of a species, usually birds, gather in a display area called a lek; females attend the lek and choose a mate.

- Females assess male fitness, basing it on 'honest' signals such a low parasite burden and good condition.

4.4 Extended response question

The activity which follows presents an extended response question similar to the style that you will encounter in the examination.

You should have a good understanding of courtship before attempting the question.

You should give your completed answer to your teacher or tutor for marking, or try to mark it yourself using the suggested marking scheme.

Extended response question: Courtship

Write an essay about courtship under the following headings:

- sexual diamorphism; *(4 marks)*
- male-male rivalry; *(1 mark)*
- sneakers; *(1 mark)*
- lekking. *(4 marks)*

....

4.5 End of topic test

End of Topic 4 test

Go online

Q10: Sexual investment in females is _____ that in males. *(1 mark)*

a) equal to
b) greater than
c) lower than

....

Q11: Which of the techniques employed by organisms to increase reproductive success are true of sessile organisms? Choose all that apply. *(1 mark)*

A) Hermaphrodism
B) Lekking
C) Long sex organs
D) Sneaking

....

Q12: Which of the following are characteristics of r-selected organisms? *(1 mark)*

a) Production of few offspring, short life spans, parental care.
b) Production of few offspring, long life spans, no parental care.
c) Production of many offspring, short life spans, no parental care.
d) Production of many offspring, long life spans, parental care.

. . . .

Q13: What is the term that is used to describe the condition where there are distinct physical differences between males and females of the same species? *(1 mark)*

. . . .

Q14: Which of the following statements best explains why females are often less conspicuous than males? *(1 mark)*

a) To reduce the chances of their being confused as males by other females.
b) To provide better camouflage when protecting their young.
c) To reduce the chances of males trying to fight them.
d) Due to a lack of energy required to look nice after producing 'costly' eggs.

. . . .

Q15: How can males that are smaller or lack weapons still gain access to females? *(1 mark)*

. . . .

Q16: Which of the following correctly identifies the term imprinting? *(1 mark)*

a) Reversible, occurs within a critical period, has no effect on choice of mate.
b) Reversible, does not occur within a critical period, can have an effect on choice of mate.
c) Irreversible, occurs within a critical period, can have an effect on choice of mate.
d) Irreversible, does not occur within a critical period, has no effect on choice of mate.

. . . .

Topic 5

The parasite niche, transmission and virulence

Contents

Prerequisite knowledge

You should already know that:

- *parasites form symbiotic relationships with hosts, where the parasite benefits at the host's detriment;*

- *ectoparasites, such as ticks, live on the surface of a host as compared to endoparasites, such as tapeworms, which live inside the host;*

- *more highly evolved parasites have indirect life cycles;*

- *parasites can be transmitted by vectors;*

- *interspecific competition occurs between organisms of two different species and can be reduced through compromising over resources.*

Learning objectives

By the end of this topic, you should be able to:

- *describe the symbiotic relationship shared by parasites and their hosts;*
- *state what is meant by a narrow niche as applied to parasites;*
- *explain what degenerate means as applied to parasites;*
- *define the terms definitive host and intermediate host;*
- *explain the term vector using examples;*
- *compare the fundamental and realised niche of parasites;*
- *explain what is meant by competitive exclusion principle and resource partitioning;*
- *describe the relationship between parasite transmission and virulence;*
- *give examples of factors that increase transmission rates of parasites;*
- *explain what is meant by the theory "The Extended Phenotype";*
- *give examples of how parasites modify their hosts for their own gain.*

5.1   The parasite niche

At least 50% of all species are parasitic, and all free-living species are thought to host parasites to some extent. A parasite forms a symbiotic relationship with the host, benefiting at the expense of the host. The parasite gains nutrients and shelter from the host. Unlike other symbiotic relationships, such as those between predator and prey, the reproductive potential of the parasite is much higher than that of its host.

An ecological niche is a complex outline of tolerances and requirements of a species. Parasites tend to have a very narrow niche due to high host specificity. As the host provides so many of the parasite's needs, many parasites are said to be degenerate, lacking in structures and organs found in other organisms. A good example of this is tapeworms, which lack a digestive system as the host has already digested the food. This degeneration is also found amongst the flatworm parasites. Flatworms such as *Fasciola Ascaris* lack organs for movement, digestion of food and sensing light as these are not required whilst inside the host. This does limit parasites, in the sense that the adult parasite will not be able to survive outside the host.

The niche for an ectoparasite is on the surface of its host, e.g. lice, ticks and leeches, whereas an endoparasite lives within the host, e.g. tapeworms, flatworms and protozoans. There are two types of host.

1. The **definitive (primary) host** where the parasite reaches sexual maturity.

2. The **intermediate (secondary) host** which the parasite might require in order to complete its life cycle, perhaps carrying out asexual reproduction to greatly increase it numbers or as a means of **transmission**, thus sometimes making the intermediate host a **vector**.

A good example of a parasite that has two hosts is the tapeworm *T. solium*, a parasite found in human intestines. Humans act as the definitive host in this case. *T. solium* has evolved to specialise and adapt to two different hosts, which is difficult and highly advanced. The advantage is that large parasites, such as the tapeworm *T. solium*, which would not be able to leave their definitive human host easily can do so via their much smaller eggs. The eggs enter pigs if they eat food contaminated with human faeces, and can then be transmitted to a new human host via undercooked pig meat. The tapeworm may further increase its numbers by carrying out asexual reproduction within the intermediate (secondary) pig host. In CfE Higher Biology, we referred to this more evolved parasite life cycle as indirect.

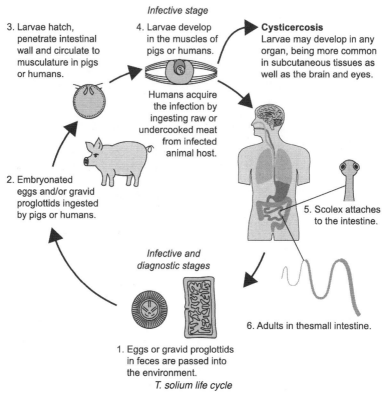

T. solium life cycle

In the image above, **gravid proglottid** refer to any segment of a tapeworm containing both male and female reproductive organs and **cysticercosis** refers to a parasitic tissue infection.

Vectors

Vectors are responsible for transmitting a parasite from one host to another, yet may also be a host for the parasite. Good examples of vectors include mosquitoes in transmitting the malaria parasite or ticks in transmitting both Lyme disease and babesiosis disease-causing parasites. Many endoparasites acquire hosts passively. The human endoparasitic nematode *Ascaris* produces vast quantities of eggs in the digestive tract that pass out in faeces. More people become infected through ingesting the eggs if there is poor sanitation and contamination of water supplies. Natural selection favours those parasites that can find and obtain nutrition from its host quickly and efficiently.

Washing clothes in or drinking this water in Tanzania will promote transmission of parasites by https://www.flickr.com/people/23116228@N07, licenced under the Creative Commons https://creativecommons.org/licenses/by/2.0/deed.en license

Ectoparasites and many endoparasites have sophisticated methods for finding new hosts. Mosquitoes, for example, initially try to locate a human host for the malaria parasite by sensing movement and then verifying that the host is human based on body temperature, exhaled carbon dioxide and chemicals on the surface of the skin.

In ecology, two niches exist.

1. The **fundamental niche** - this is the niche that the organism occupies when there are no other species present competing for space or resources.

2. The **realised niche** is the niche that the organism occupies when there is competition from other species.

Competitive exclusion principle is when two species are in intense competition with one another, thus the niches occupied by each are very similar - the weaker of the two species will likely die out, becoming extinct in that area.

Resource partitioning is where two competing species occupy different realised niches, compromising over resources and thus managing to exist simultaneously. These terms and concepts can be applied to parasite niches as well as any other species.

Nematode species	Section of the intestine inhabited (%)
Passalurus ambiguus	8-25
Obeliscoides cuniculi	19-37
Trichuris leporis	30-52
Dirofilaria scapiceps	45-68
Bayliascaris procyonis	62-88

Range of rabbit intestine occupied by five different nematode species

The table shows five different species of nematode parasite found in the intestines of rabbits. To reduce competition, each has specialised to position itself at a certain area of the intestinal tract. For example, *Passalurus ambiguus* inhabits the first 8-25% of the intestine. It overlaps slightly with *Obeliscoides cuniculi*, which can be found from 19% along the tract to 37%. This will involve adapting to the different environmental conditions, such as nutrient availability and pH level. They are said to have effectively carried out resource partitioning.

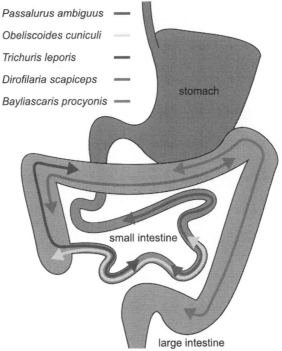

Fundamental and realised niches of nematodes in intestines

The parasite niche of Clostridium difficile

C. difficile is a bacterial species that lives in the large intestine of humans and is transmitted via spores produced and spread in faeces. Initial symptoms include very bad diarrhoea. High risk patients are those on antibiotics who are currently under medical care in hospitals, nursing homes, outpatient surgery centres or health centres. Antibiotics are used to kill bacterial infections. It is therefore unavoidable that they kill the harmless bacteria with which we share a positive symbiotic relationship, including those that live in the gut. This leaves a niche open for harmful *C. difficile* bacteria to fill.

The parasite niche: Activity

Q1: Match the terms with their definitions.

Go online

Fundamental niche:	two different species compromise over resources to reduce competition.
Realised niche:	competition between two species will see local extinction of the weaker.
Resource partitioning:	required by some parasites to complete their life cycle.
Competitive exclusion principle:	where the parasite reaches sexual maturity.
Vector:	exists in the absence of interspecific competition.
Definitive host:	exists in the presence of interspecific competition.
Intermediate host:	responsible for parasite transmission.

. . . .

5.2   Transmission and virulence

Transmission is the spread of a parasite to a host. **Virulence** is the deleterious effect that the parasite has on the host.

The rule is that, the higher the transmission rate, the greater the virulence.

Transmission rates are greatest when there is:

- overcrowding of hosts, such as in places with very high population density;
- a means of transmission such as presence of **vectors**, e.g. mosquitoes, or water for **waterborne** parasites, e.g. cholera.

The extended phenotype

Parasites that can maximise transmission are favoured by natural selection. The most successful parasites have adapted means to exploit and change host behaviour in order to increase transmission. In effect, the parasite or virus 'makes' the host behave in such a way that transmission of the disease is increased. This concept was referred to as "The Extended Phenotype" in a book by Richard Dawkins. A number of host behaviours may be altered:

- foraging;
- movement;
- sexual behaviour;
- habitat choice;
- anti-predator behaviour.

In these cases, this modified host behaviour is said to become part of the **extended phenotype** of the parasite. Some fish-harbouring parasites have been observed hiding or feeding at night, which is not characteristic of their normal behaviour. This anti-predator behaviour is believed to be an extension of the parasite. Clearly, if the host survives, so too does the parasite. By foraging at night, the host is less likely to be preyed upon, thus increasing their chance of survival.

Another good example of this hypothesised extended phenotype is coughing and sneezing when you have a cold. Some theorise that this is an extension of the cold virus in an effort to increase transmission. There are numerous examples of modified animal behaviour which seems to have no benefit to the host, yet is advantageous to the parasite. By manipulating the host's behaviour, the parasite increases its own fitness. Others believe that those with certain sexually transmitted infections may experience increased sexual behaviour for the same reason. Parasites are also capable of suppressing the host's immune system, modifying host size and reproductive rate in ways that benefit the growth, reproduction or transmission of the parasite. A larger sized host will result in a greater number of spores. Furthermore, if a host reproduces less often, they may conserve energy that the parasite can use.

Transmission and virulence: Questions

Go online

Virulence refers to the percentage of infections that result in death. The following table presents information about the number of cases of the disease toxocariasis in foxes and the number that resulted in the death of the fox. This disease has been monitored over recent years because it is the most likely disease affecting foxes that could be transmitted to humans.

Year	Number of reported toxocariasis cases	Number of infections resulting in fox death
2010	13	8
2011	56	50
2012	144	75
2013	95	70
2014	25	15

Q2: Calculate the percentage change in number of reported cases from 2011 to 2012.

....

Q3: In which year was toxocariasis most virulent?

a) 2010
b) 2011
c) 2012
d) 2013
e) 2014

....

Q4: In which year was toxocariasis least virulent?

a) 2010
b) 2011
c) 2012
d) 2013
e) 2014

....

Q5: Summer 2011 was particularly warm with plenty of rabbits and small rodents available for foxes to feed on. Knowing what you do about the factors that increase parasite transmission, suggest why 2012 saw the greatest number of reported toxocariasis cases.

....

5.3 Learning points

Summary

- Parasites have a narrow niche due to high host specificity.

- Parasites are said to be degenerate due to the absence of certain structures and organs.

- Ectoparasites live on the surface of their host, whereas endoparasites live inside their host.

- The definitive or primary host is the host where the parasite reaches sexual maturity.

- In the case of indirect life cycles, some parasites also have a secondary or intermediate host that is used in transmission or where an asexual phase of their life cycle may occur.

- Indirect life cycles are highly evolved and greatly increase parasite success.

- Vectors, such as insects, or water transmit parasites.

- The fundamental niche is the parasite's niche in the absence of interspecific competition.

- The realised niche is the parasite's niche in the present of interspecific competition.

- When interspecific competition occurs between species with very similar niches, usually one of the two species becomes locally extinct.

- If the two species can compromise over resources by means of resource partitioning, both may co-exist.

- Higher rates of parasite transmission are linked to higher virulence.

- Transmission can be increased in overcrowded regions and where vectors are available. Parasites are said to modify host behaviour to increase transmission by altering host foraging behaviour, anti-predator behaviour, sexual behaviour, movement and habitat choice.

- These modifications are said to be an extension of the parasite's phenotype in a theory known as "The Extended Phenotype".

- Parasites also suppress host immune responses, and modify host size and reproduction for their own benefit.

5.4 Extended response question

The activity which follows presents an extended response question similar to the style that you will encounter in the examination.

You should have a good understanding of parasite niche before attempting the question.

You should give your completed answer to your teacher or tutor for marking, or try to mark it yourself using the suggested marking scheme.

Extended response question: Parasite niche

Discuss the concept of the parasite niche. *(10 marks)*

. . . .

5.5 End of topic test

End of Topic 5 test

Parasites and hosts form a symbiotic relationship.

Go online

Q6: This relationship is of _____ to the parasite. *(1 mark)*

a) benefit
b) detriment

. . . .

Q7: This relationship is of _____ to the host. *(1 mark)*

a) benefit
b) detriment

. . . .

Q8: Parasites have a _____ niche. *(1 mark)*

a) narrow
b) wide

. . . .

Q9: This is due to _____ host specificity. *(1 mark)*

a) high
b) low

. . . .

Q10: Tapeworms tend to lack a digestive system. What word that describes tapeworms and many parasites could be used here? *(1 mark)*

....

Q11: Liver flukes that reach sexual maturity in the livers of goats carry out asexual reproduction in snails as part of their life cycle. What term is used to describe the snail? *(1 mark)*

....

Q12: What term is used to describe the goat in the context of the previous question? *(1 mark)*

....

Q13: *Obeliscoides cuniculi* and *Trichuris leporis* are two species of tapeworm that parasitise rabbit intestines. Their niches are too similar and *Trichuris leporis* becomes locally extinct. What term describes this? *(1 mark)*

....

Q14: *Passalurus ambiguus* and *Dirofilaria scapiceps* are two other species of tapeworm that parasitise rabbit intestines. They are able to co-exist. What term describes this? *(1 mark)*

....

Q15: Which of the following statements that refer to nematode parasites are examples of parasites in their realised niche? Choose all that apply. *(1 mark)*

  A) The nematode *Ascaris* inhabits the full length of the human intestine as it is not under any competition from other nematode species.
  B) The nematode *Acsaris* inhabits the first 20% of the human intestine and the nematode *Strongyloides* inhabits the last 20% of the human intestine.
  C) The mouse parasites *Heligmosomoides polygyrus*, found in the stomach, and *Litomosoides sigmodontis*, found in the small intestine, have adapted to suit different pH environments, thus reducing competition for resources.

....

Q16: Which of the following statements relating to parasites best describes the extended phenotype? *(1 mark)*

a) Degenerate
b) Modification of host behaviour
c) Transmitted by vectors
d) Virulence

....

....

Topic 6

Immune response to parasites

Contents

Prerequisite knowledge

You should already know that:

- *the body may defend attack using non-specific and specific means;*

- *white blood cells provide cellular defence against foreign antigens;*

- *antibodies are special proteins produced during immune responsees.*

Learning objectives

By the end of this topic, you should be able to:

- give examples of physical and chemical barriers in non-specific defence;
- describe inflammatory response and explain its role in non-specific defence;
- describe the process of phagocytosis and the role of phagocytes in this process;
- state the role of natural killer cells in non-specific defence;
- describe the role of phagocytes in specific defence;
- compare the role of T and B lymphocytes in specific defence;
- explain what clonal selection is and its role in immunological memory;
- discuss how endoparasites can evade detection by the host's immune system;
- explain how antigenic variation allows parasites to remain a step ahead of the host's immune response;
- define the term epidemiology;
- describe what herd immunity is;
- define the term herd immunity threshold.

6.1 Non-specific defence

Immune response to parasites

Mammals have innate or natural, non-specific defences to parasites (which includes disease causing bacteria and viruses). Physical barriers include:

- skin;

- chemical secretions, including mucus, tears and stomach acid;

- **inflammatory response**;

- **phagocytes** (white blood cells);

- **natural killer cells** - lymphocytes (white blood cells) responsible for destroying abnormal cells.

Should this defence ultimately fail, mammals are armed with specific or adaptive cellular defence involving immune surveillance by white blood cells.

Inflammatory response

When the skin is damaged, perhaps by a cut or wound, the external barrier to parasites is broken. Parasites may enter and this triggers localised inflammatory response. The wounded region becomes warmer and redder as a result of small blood vessels dilating. This increases blood flow to the injured area, thus increasing the number of white blood cells, such as phagocytes, allowing a suitable defence or attack so that healing can begin.

Phagocytes

Phagocytes are white blood cells with a non-specific role in defence. Phagocytes arrive at the site of infection and engulf parasites by enfolding their plasma membrane around the parasite. The parasite is then brought into the phagocyte in a vacuole or vesicle. Phagocytes contain special organelles called lysosomes. These are filled with digestive enzymes. The lysosomes fuse with the vacuole, releasing the digestive enzymes and allowing the enzymes to digest the parasite. The following depicts the process of **phagocytosis**.

Go online

Phagocytosis

Phagocyte is attracted to chemical signals produced by a bacterium. 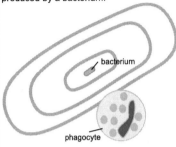	Vacuole forms around the bacterium. Lysosomes move towards and fuse with the vacuole. 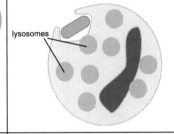
Lysosomes release digestive enzymes into the vacuole, the bacterium is broken down by enzymes. 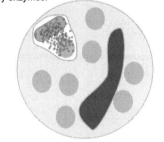	Vacuole disintegrates releasing disgested products into the cytoplasm of the phagocyte. 

Go online

Non-specific defence: Activity

Q1: Arrange the following steps in phagocytosis in the correct order.

- The parasite is digested.
- Parasite is brought into the phagocyte in a vacuole.
- Phagocytes move to the site of injury.
- Lysosomes fuse with the vacuole releasing digestive enzymes.
- Plasma membrane of the phagocyte engulfs the parasite.
- Lysosomes move towards the vacuole.

6.2 Specific defence

Specific defence is carried out by white blood cells. White blood cells carry out **immune surveillance**.

Phagocytes

Phagocytes also have a role in specific defence. Foreign antigens, previously engulfed by phagocytes, are pushed back out onto the surface of the phagocyte. The phagocyte then presents these antigens to lymphocytes, another type of white blood cell.

Lymphocytes

Lymphocytes are part of a specific response, with a different lymphocyte produced in response to each type of foreign antigen.

Mammals are armed with two types of lymphocytes:

- **B lymphocytes** also known as B cells;
- **T lymphocytes** also known as T cells.

Both types circulate throughout the blood, and recognise specific foreign antigens. Antigens are proteins on the surface of all cells. If these antigens do not belong to the host, they are considered foreign. These include foreign molecules belonging to bacteria, viruses, fungi, parasitic worms and cells from transplanted tissues.

B lymphocytes

In response to the foreign antigens presented by phagocytes, B cells produce proteins called antibodies that are specific in shape to the antigen.

T lymphocytes

T cells work by destroying specific infected or damaged cells by bringing about **apoptosis** (cell death).

Clonal selection

Both B and T lymphocytes carry out **clonal selection**. Clonal selection is process by which lymphocytes become amplified undergoing the process of mitosis. Each type of lymphocyte divides and differentiates into two clones. One clone becomes a plasma cell, working to combat the antigen and is therefore only short lived. In comparison, the other clone lives significantly longer assuming the role of a **memory cell**. Should the individual be exposed to a particular parasite a second time, B lymphocyte memory cells very quickly mount a defence producing the specific antibody required to combat the antigen. In such cases the individual would express no symptoms whatsoever.

Go online

Clonal selection of B lymphocytes

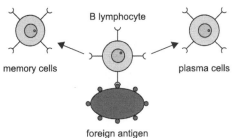

When a foreign antigen enters the body, the B lymphocyte that contains the antibody receptor that is specific to the antigen binds to it. The B lymphocyte then undergoes mitosis to produce many daughter cells, which then develop into either memory cells or plasma cells.

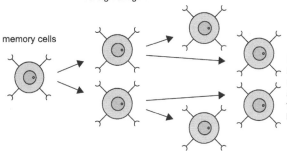

Having undergone mitosis, there are many copies of the antibody specific to the antigen in the body.

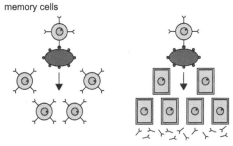

Memory cells recognise the antigen if it enters the body again and they initiate the secondary immune response. Since there are many memory cells in the body, antibody-secreting plasma cells can be produced rapidly to destroy the foreign antigen.

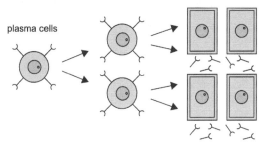

The B lymphocytes that develop into plasma cells secrete antibodies in response to foreign antigens. These antibodies are specific to the antigen detected and destroy it.

. . . .

Endoparasite Success

So why don't endoparasites stimulate an immune response from mammals since their cells will contain foreign antigens?

Endoparasites mimic host antigens, therefore remaining undetected by the host's immune system. Endoparasites are also capable of modifying the host-immune response, preventing the host from mounting an attack so the parasite remains alive.

Some parasites show a huge **antigenic variation**. This promotes a rapid evolution rate, and the parasite remains a step ahead of host immune cell clonal selection. This is why flu is so successful. Flu has evolved over generations so that there are many forms, and being immune to one form does not guarantee immunity to other types.

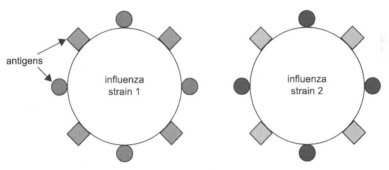

Compare the antigens of the two influenza strains here. Memory cells from strain 1 would provide no immune response to an attack from strain 2.

Epidemiology

Epidemiology is the study of the outbreak and spread of infectious diseases. Diseases spread more quickly through dense populations and areas of overcrowding. In every population, as a result of genetic variation, some individuals will be genetically immune to a disease. Since diseases are transmitted from individual to individual, resistant individuals will present a barrier to transmission. If this number of resistant individuals is high enough, an epidemic may be avoided. These resistant individuals are ultimately providing a level of protection to non-immune members of the population. This conferred protection is known as **herd immunity** or community immunity. The **herd immunity threshold** is the density of resistant hosts in the population required to prevent an epidemic. The number of resistant individuals in a population may be increased by means of vaccinations. This herd immunity would provide some protection to non-vaccinated individuals.

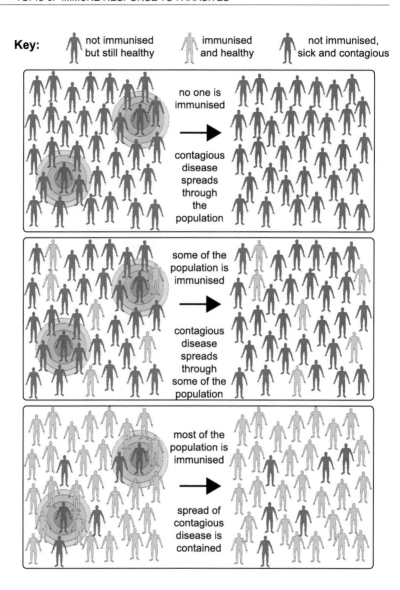

Specific defence: Questions

The following table provides data about immune response to chicken pox.

Go online

Time (days following infection)	Volume of chicken pox antigen (μg/ml)	Volume of antibody (μg/ml)
0	50	0
2	140.5	0
4	220	0
6	150	240
8	130.5	360
10	50	380
12	20	380

Q2: Present the information in the table as a line graph.

. . . .

Q3: Use values from the table to describe the volume of chicken pox antigen over the 12 days.

. . . .

Q4: Describe the volume of antibody over the 12 days.

. . . .

The individual is exposed to chicken pox a second time. The graph below shows the levels of chicken pox antigen and antibody levels this time.

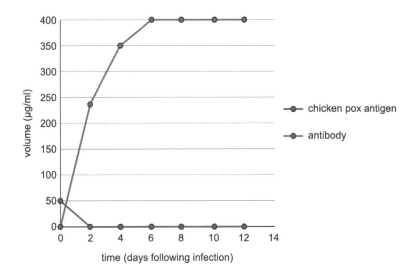

Q5: Explain the volumes of chicken pox antigens and antibody over the 12 days following infection.

. . . .

. . . .

6.3 Learning points

Summary

- Mammals are armed with non-specific defences to parasite attack. The skin provides a physical barrier, and mucus, saliva, tears and stomach acid all provide chemical barriers.

- Inflammatory response is a non-specific defences that increases the blood flow to an injured area.

- Phagocytes provide non-specific defence by engulfing foreign antigens into a vacuole. Special organelles called lysosomes then fuse with the vacuole releasing digestive enzymes to digest the antigen.

- Natural killer cells are white blood cells that destroy abnormal cells by bringing about apoptosis.

- Phagocytes also have a role in specific defence, by presenting foreign antigens to lymphocytes.

- Specific lymphocytes are produced in response to specific antigens.

- B lymphocytes produce specific antibodies to combat specific foreign antigens.

- T lymphocytes target infected or damaged cells and bring about apoptosis.

- Lymphocytes are amplified through mitosis. This is called clonal selection. Some clones are used in combating the attack. Others become immunological memory cells.

- Endoparasites are able to mimic host antigens and avoid destruction.

- Many parasites show vast antigenic variation. This means being immune to one strain does not confer immunity to other strains.

- Epidemiology is the study of outbreak and spread of infection diseases.

- Herd immunity is the protection offered to susceptible individuals by resistant individuals within the population.

- The herd immunity threshold is the density of resistant hosts in the population required to prevent an epidemic.

6.4   Extended response question

The activity which follows presents an extended response question similar to the style that you will encounter in the examination.

You should have a good understanding of immune responses before attempting the question.

You should give your completed answer to your teacher or tutor for marking, or try to mark it yourself using the suggested marking scheme.

Extended response question: Immune responses

Describe how mammals use immune responses to reduce the effects of parasites. *(10 marks)*

. . . .

6.5   End of topic test

End of Topic 6 test

Q6:   Complete the table using the statements listed. *(4 marks)*

Go online

Non-specific defence	Specific defence

Statement list: Action by B cells, Action by T cells, Clonal selection, Inflammatory response, Mucus, Phagocytes present antigens, Phagocytosis, Skin.

. . . .

Q7:   During phagocytosis, special organelles release digestive _ _ _ _ _ _ _ _ into the vacuole containing the parasite. *(1 mark)*

. . . .

Q8:   What are the special organelles from the previous question known as? *(1 mark)*

. . . .

Q9:   In response to parasitic attack, lymphocytes are amplified through mitosis. What is this cellular response known as? *(1 mark)*

....

Q10: The role of T lymphocytes in immune response is in: *(1 mark)*

a) phagocytosis.
b) clonal selection.
c) production of specific antibodies.
d) apoptosis of specific damaged cells.

....

Q11: Which of the following best describes how endoparasites evade destruction? *(1 mark)*

a) Mimics host antigens.
b) Mimics other parasites.
c) Kills lymphocytes.
d) Kills phagocytes.

....

Q12: Due to antigenic variation, last season's flu vaccine _____ be effective against this season's strain. *(1 mark)*

a) will
b) will not

....

Q13: NHS Scotland plans to vaccinate preschool children against mumps, measles and rubella using the MMR vaccination. Some parents are reluctant to vaccinate, being aware that if enough other children get vaccinated, their child will receive some protection anyway.

What is the ability to receive some protection even without having been vaccinated known as? *(1 mark)*

....

Q14: What is the study of outbreaks and spread of disease called? *(1 mark)*

....

Topic 7

Parasitic life cycles and viruses

Contents

Prerequisite knowledge

You should already know that:

- *some methods by which parasites are transmitted include direct contact, consumption of secondary hosts and vectors;*

- *malaria is an example of a human disease caused by a parasite;*

- *DNA codes for proteins;*

- *during the process of protein synthesis, DNA is transcribed into a molecule of mRNA which is then translated into a polypeptide strand that is further modified into a functional protein.*

Learning objectives

By the end of this topic, you should be able to:

- *name common parasites;*
- *state, with examples, that many parasites require more than one host to complete their life cycle;*
- *give examples of parasites that are responsible for causing human diseases;*
- *describe how ectoparasites and endoparasites of the body cavities are transmitted;*
- *describe how endoparasites of the body tissues are transmitted;*
- *give examples of parasites that can complete their life cycle within one host;*
- *give examples of human diseases caused by bacteria and viruses;*
- *state what a virus is and describe its structure;*
- *state that the outer surface of a virus contains antigens that a host cell may or may not be able to detect as foreign;*
- *explain the role of the lipid membrane envelope around some viruses and state what it is derived from;*
- *describe the process of virus replication;*
- *define the term retrovirus;*
- *explain how retroviruses replicate compared to viruses.*

7.1   Parasitic life cycles

Common parasites include:

- protists - single celled organisms, e.g. **amoebas**;

- platyhelminths - flatworms;

- nematodes - roundworms;

- arthropods - invertebrates with jointed legs, segmented bodies and an exoskeleton, e.g. ticks;

- bacteria;

- viruses.

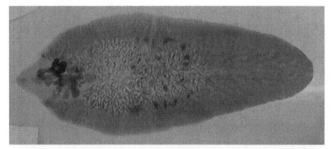

Fasciola hepatica - parasitic liver fluke, member of the platyhelminthes

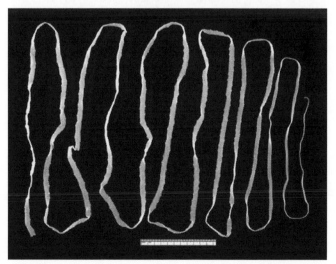

Adult Taenia saginata tapeworm, another member of the platyhelminthes

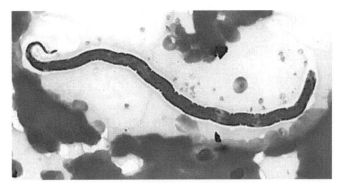

Loa loa - parasitic nematode worm

Ectoparasite - tick

Transmission

Ectoparasites such as ticks and lice are usually transmitted from host to host via direct contact.

Endoparasites of the main body cavities, such as the gut, may also be transmitted by direct contact, often caused by poor hygiene, e.g. transmitting tapeworm eggs after scratching or touching the skin around the anus and not washing hands properly. Endoparasites of the gut are also transmitted through consumption of secondary hosts, e.g. humans consuming undercooked pork may be at risk from the tapeworm *T. solium*.

Endoparasites of the body tissues are usually transmitted by vectors. Freshwater snails act as vectors for liver flukes that affect the liver and gall bladder of sheep and goats. Similarly, horse flies transmit *Loa loa*, a roundworm responsible for affecting connective tissue, skin and eyes in humans.

Human diseases caused by parasites

Several human diseases are caused by parasites. Perhaps two of the best known are:

1. **schistosomiasis** - also known as bilharzias. This disease is caused by flatworms
   of the *Schistosoma* species which live in fresh water in sub-tropical and tropical
   regions of the world. Presenting as a skin rash and cough, this is readily treatable
   in the UK.

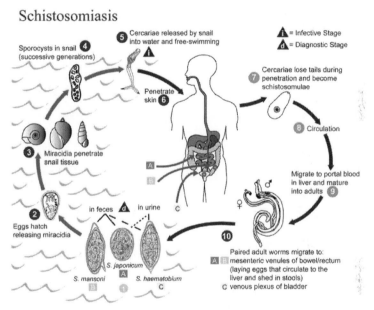

Schistosomiasis life cycle

2. **malaria** - a serious tropical disease spread by mosquitoes that are infected with
   the malaria parasite *Plasmodium* of which there are several different species.
   Presenting as a headache and fever, this is treatable if detected early enough.
   If treatment is not strong enough, malaria can recur. Sometimes, the parasite
   can exist in a dormant state, often hiding in the liver cells so is undetected by the
   body's immune system, allowing future recurrence. In the *Plasmodium falciparum*,
   the parasite has adhesive proteins on its surface, allowing it to stick to the inner
   wall of the blood vessels. This also allows it to remain undetected by the immune
   system.

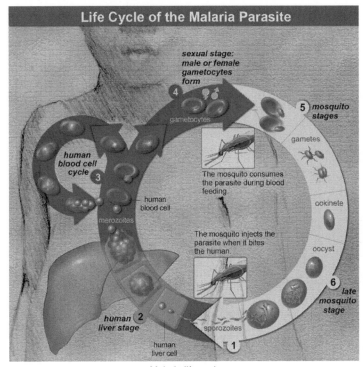

Malaria life cycle

Both of these parasites require more than one host to complete their life cycle. In the case of malaria, the parasite grows and multiplies inside the human host. The female mosquito acts as a second host, not only responsible for transmitting the parasite, but also for allowing growth and multiplication of the parasite when in a stage known as the blood stage. *Schistosoma* flatworms also have two hosts: some freshwater snails and humans. Infectious parasites leave the snail host, entering freshwater. Any human swimming in infected water may become infected when the skin comes in contact with the water.

Other human diseases can complete their life cycle within one host.

1. Ectoparasitic arthropods, e.g. ticks.

2. Endoparasitic protists, e.g. amoebas.

3. Bacteria, e.g. tuberculosis.

4. Viruses, e.g. influenza and HIV.

Parasitic life cycles: Questions

Decide which of the following statements about parasitic life cycles are true and which are false.

Go online

In the case of a false statement, how should the *italicised* part be changed to form a true statement? Provide a suitable correction.

Q1: Amoebas are *multi-celled* parasites.

a) True
b) False

....

Q2: Correction:

....

Q3: Ectoparasites are transmitted via *direct contact*.

a) True
b) False

....

Q4: Correction:

....

Q5: Platyhelminthes are the *roundworms*.

a) True
b) False

....

Q6: Correction:

....

Q7: Endoparasites of the body tissues are often transmitted via *direct contact*.

a) True
b) False

....

Q8: Correction:

....

Q9: A malaria parasite which requires both human and mosquito hosts to complete its life cycle is:

a) an arthropod tick.
b) *Plasmodium.*
c) *Schistosoma.*

....

Q10: A platyhelminthes parasite which requires both human and freshwater snail hosts to complete its life cycle is:

a) an arthropod tick.
b) *Plasmodium.*
c) *Schistosoma.*

....

Q11: A parasite with jointed legs, segmented body and exoskeleton, capable of completing its life cycle on a single host is:

a) an arthropod tick.
b) *Plasmodium.*
c) *Schistosoma.*

....

The unicellular parasite *Trypanosoma brucei* attacks the human nervous system causing sleeping sickness which is a common condition in regions of the world such as Africa where tsetse flies are found. *Trypanosoma brucei* contains variant surface glycoprotein coats which are so thick that the immune system of the host cannot access the plasma membrane of the parasite. In addition, the parasite undergoes regular antigenic variation. The following flow chart shows the life cycle of *Trypanosoma brucei*.

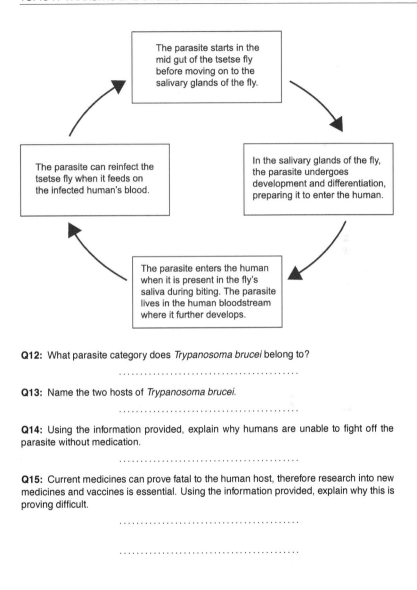

Q12: What parasite category does *Trypanosoma brucei* belong to?

. . . .

Q13: Name the two hosts of *Trypanosoma brucei*.

. . . .

Q14: Using the information provided, explain why humans are unable to fight off the parasite without medication.

. . . .

Q15: Current medicines can prove fatal to the human host, therefore research into new medicines and vaccines is essential. Using the information provided, explain why this is proving difficult.

. . . .

. . . .

7.2   Viruses

Viruses are tiny (20-400 nm) infectious agents that can only replicate inside a host cell. Viruses contain genetic material in the form of DNA or RNA, packaged in a protective protein coat as shown in the picture of the **bacteriophage**. A bacteriophage is a virus that uses a bacterium as a host cell. The outer surface of a virus contains antigens that, in some cases, the host cell may not be able to detect as foreign.

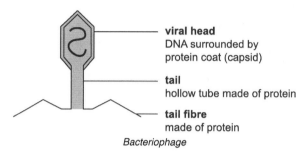

viral head
DNA surrounded by protein coat (capsid)

tail
hollow tube made of protein

tail fibre
made of protein

Bacteriophage

Lipid membrane

The protein coat of some viruses is surrounded by a lipid membrane envelope. This envelope is composed of the host cell's materials. It is thought that the envelope has a role in allowing the virus to attach to the host and gain entry. It may also help the virus avoid detection by the host cell.

Replication of a virus

Viral replication has the following steps.

1. Virus attaches to the surface of the host cell.

2. Virus injects its DNA or RNA into the host cell.

3. Virus interrupts the host cell's own metabolism, often entering the host's genome.

4. Virus uses the host cell's machinery and raw materials to replicate the DNA.

5. Again, using the host cell's resources, the DNA is transcribed into mRNA then translated into protein so more viral protein coats are produced.

6. The new DNA then enters the newly formed protein coats, thus producing many new viruses.

7. These then leave the cell to infect new cells and the host cell undergoes **lysis**, bursting.

Viral replication

Go online

viral particle

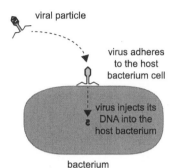

virus adheres
to the host
bacterium cell

virus injects its
DNA into the
host bacterium

bacterium

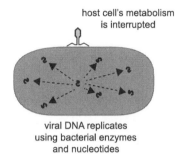

host cell's metabolism
is interrupted

viral DNA replicates
using bacterial enzymes
and nucleotides

viral DNA is transcribed
into mRNA and translated
into viral protein coats by
the bacterium

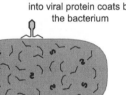

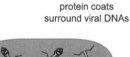

protein coats
surround viral DNAs

host bacterium
breaks up (lysis)

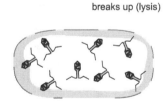

viral particles released
to infect othe cells

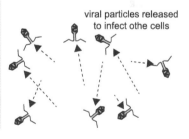

Retroviruses

Retroviruses are viruses with RNA rather than DNA. HIV is a good example of retrovirus. On injecting their RNA into the host cell, they also inject the enzyme **reverse transcriptase** to first synthesise DNA from the single-stranded RNA. This new DNA is then inserted into the genome of the host cell. As part of the host's DNA, the virus's genes can then be transcribed, ultimately synthesising new viral particles.

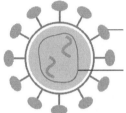

glycoprotein on membrane envelope
binds receptor on T helper cell

capsid
contains two single-stranded RNA
molecules and two molecules of
the enzyme reverse transcriptase

HIV virus structure

A glycoprotein on the surface of the HIV envelope binds to a specific receptor on the surface of a helper T cell. Leaving its envelope behind at the cell membrane, the viral particle enters the host T cell. The capsid proteins are removed by enzymes. Viral reverse transcriptase catalyses the synthesis of a DNA strand complementary to the viral RNA template. A complementary DNA strand is synthesised and the double stranded DNA is incorporated into the host's genome. Viral genes are transcribed into mRNA to make new viral genomes. The mRNA is also translated into HIV proteins in the cytoplasm. New viral particles are assembled. As each viral particle buds out of the host cell it is coated by a membranous envelope.

Retroviruses and evolution in eukaryotes

The genomes of most eukaryotic species contain a high proportion of **retrotransposons**. Retroviruses are thought to be the origin of these retrotransposons. The great variability of vertebrate antibodies is hypothesised to have evolved from retrotranposons.

Go online

Replication of a retrovirus: Activity

Q16: Complete the diagram using the labels listed.

RNA	$\rightarrow$		$\rightarrow$	
-		-		-

Label list: **DNA**, host RNA polymerase, **RNA**, viral reverse transcriptase.

. . . .

7.3 Learning points

Summary

- Common parasites include protists, platyhelminthes, nematodes, ectoparasitic arthropods, bacteria and viruses.

- Ectoparasites are transmitted via direct contact.

- Endoparasites of the body cavities are transmitted via direct contact or consumption of secondary hosts.

- Endoparasites of the body tissues are transmitted via vectors.

- Schistosomiasis and malaria are examples of human diseases caused by parasites.

- *Plasmodium* species and *Schistosoma* species require two hosts to complete their life cycles.

- Other parasites can complete their life cycle within one host. Examples include endoparasitic amoebas and ectoparasitic ticks.

- Tuberculosis is a human disease caused by bacteria while influenza and HIV are human diseases caused by viruses.

- Many bacteria and viruses can complete their life cycles within a single host.

- Viruses are composed of nucleic acid enclosed inside a protein coat.

- The outer surface of a virus contains antigens that a host cell may or may not be able to detect as foreign.

- Some viruses are further surrounded by a lipid membrane, composed of the host's materials.

- The lipid surround is thought to aid the virus in remaining undetected inside the host cell.

- Retroviruses are viruses that contain RNA as their genetic material rather than DNA. HIV is an example of a retrovirus.

- RNA retroviruses use the enzyme reverse transcriptase to first produce DNA, which is then inserted into the genome of the host cell. These virus genes form new viral particles when transcribed inside the host.

7.4   End of topic test

End of Topic 7 test

Go online

Q17: Name four groups of common parasites. *(4 marks)*

....

Q18: Ectoparasites are transmitted via _____ contact. *(1 mark)*

a) direct
b) indirect

....

Q19: Endoparasites of the body cavity are transmitted via _____ contact. *(1 mark)*

a) direct
b) indirect

....

Q20: Endoparasites of the body cavity are also transmitted via: *(1 mark)*

a) secondary hosts.
b) vectors.

....

Q21: Endoparasites of the body tissues are transmitted via: *(1 mark)*

a) secondary hosts.
b) vectors.

....

Q22: Name two human diseases caused by parasites that require a second host. *(2 marks)*

....

Q23: Tuberculosis is a human disease that only requires a single host. What group of parasites is it caused by? *(1 mark)*

....

Q24: HIV and influenza are human diseases. What group of parasites are they caused by? *(1 mark)*

....

Q25: The size range of viruses is 20-400 __. *(1 mark)*

a) nm
b) μm
c) mm
d) cm

....

Q26: Which of the following can be components of a virus? *(3 marks)*

1. Internal carbohydrates
2. Lipid coat
3. Nucleus
4. Protein coat
5. RNA

....

Q27: Which of the following statements are true of the lipid membrane surround found in some viruses? *(2 marks)*

1. They are composed of the virus's materials.
2. They are composed of the host's materials.
3. They help the host detect the virus.
4. They help the virus remain undetected.

....

Q28: What is the name of the enzyme used by retroviruses to synthesis DNA from their RNA? *(1 mark)*

....

Q29: Arrange the steps of the replication of a virus in the correct order. *(1 mark)*

A) Virus uses the host cell's machinery and raw materials to replicate its DNA and synthesise protein coat.
B) Virus injects its DNA into the host cell.
C) These then leave the cell to infect new cells and the host cell undergoes lysis, bursting.
D) Virus interrupts the host cell's own metabolism, often entering the host's genome.
E) Virus attaches to the surface of the host cell.
F) The new DNA then enters the newly formed protein coats, thus producing many new viruses.

....

....

Topic 8

Challenges in treatment and control

Contents

Prerequisite knowledge

You should already know that:

- *vaccines and drugs are being used and continue to be developed to treat illness;*

- *overcrowding and poor sanitation are linked to rapid spread of parasites.*

Learning objectives

By the end of this topic, you should be able to:

- *state that vaccine design and drug development are both difficulties that need to be overcome in the fight against parasites;*

- *state that culturing some parasites in the laboratory is difficult and may act as a barrier to learning how to control them;*

- *explain that rapid change in parasite antigens adds to the challenge of vaccine and drug development;*

- *state that host and parasite metabolisms being so similar adds challenges to finding treatments that only target the parasite;*

- *state that improving sanitation and controlling vectors will help control parasites;*

- *explain why parasites are more prevalent and difficult to control in developing countries, tropical climates or areas affected by natural disasters;*

- *understand that controlling parasites will reduce child mortality in developing countries and that this will result in population-wide improvements.*

8.1   Challenges in treatment and control

There are many challenges to overcome in the successful treatment and control of parasites.

1. Some parasites are difficult to culture in the laboratory, so working with them to learn more about fighting them is a battle.

2. Many parasites show rapid evolution rates, often due to short generation times. This means that their **antigens** change quickly in structure. A good example is the influenza virus. There are many strains, each with different antigens. This means that designing vaccines for some parasites is almost impossible and can be expensive. In the case of influenza, UK scientists have been very successful in terms of designing vaccines and immunising many vulnerable individuals in the population. However, individuals must be vaccinated annually due to the rapid change in influenza antigen structure. For other parasites, there has been less success. Where research and development is too expensive, research into vaccines against particular parasites must be suspended.

3. Host and parasite metabolisms are extremely similar and intricately connected. Many parasites modify the host's metabolism and, in the case of viruses, their DNA becomes part of the host cell's genome. This means that tailoring drugs to fight the parasite without harming the host is extremely difficult.

Sanitation

In the UK, we have won the battle against certain parasites which other countries have not. We have **civil engineering** projects to thank for this, including sewage systems that use microbes to break down sewage into harmless products. This allows us to eradicate many diseases, such as cholera and dysentery, that are still common in poorer or less technologically advanced countries which have poor **sanitation**.

Vector Control

Another solution is coordinated vector control, killing the carrier, however this has proved controversial. In the 1950's, the pesticide DDT, also called Agent Orange, was used to kill malaria carrying mosquitoes. The disadvantage is that DDT is persistent and has subsequently bio-accumulated throughout food chains. The ultimate effect has been noted in bird of prey populations where, due to thinning eggs, numbers have fallen. Thinning eggs has been linked to the rather magnified levels of DDT in birds of prey that are in food chains containing mosquitoes.

Conditions that promote spread of parasites

Unfortunately, parasites spread most rapidly in those conditions where coordinated treatment and control programmes are most difficult to achieve. Often the most vulnerable people are affected, such as those who live in war torn regions or places affected by natural disasters.

- War - creates millions of refugees. People flee their homes and seek refuge in refugee camps. Camps become overcrowded and sanitation poor. This creates perfect conditions for rapid spread of parasites. Furthermore, reaching these refugee camps with resources to control parasites can be difficult if not impossible.

- Natural disasters - often destroy homes and sewage plants.   Clean running water and sewage treatment cease, thus creating perfect conditions for spread of parasites.

- Tropical climates - parasites are more abundant in the tropical climates that are found in many developing countries. This is because tropical climates promote large populations of insect vectors that would need to hibernate during cooler seasons in colder climates.

Improvements in parasite control

As parasite control increases, child mortality decreases. Children are able to thrive in areas where parasites are under control. Thriving children have greater opportunities for growth, development and intelligence. More intelligent, healthy children will gradually become better educated, thus sustaining control of parasites into the future. Countries will only be able to sustain the fight against parasites if they have the education and tools, rather than relying on charities and support from developed countries.

Challenges in treatment and control: Questions

The following table provides data regarding four different countries.

Go online

Country	Sanitation	Climate	Population density (per km²)
1	Improved over recent years - basic sewage systems and running water.	Sub-tropical, with a high chance of hurricanes.	6200
2	Excellent - civil engineering strong.	Temperate, with some stormy winter weather.	2500
3	Very poor - water obtained from local rivers where clothes are washed.	Tropical, with high chance of typhoons.	7100
4	Education of local people has coincided with an improvement in sanitation - sewage facilities are being developed.	Sub-tropical, with seasonal heavy rains.	3000

Three hypotheses based on the above data are:

1. Country 1 will have the highest parasite abundance.

2. Country 2 will have the lowest parasite abundance.

3. Countries 3 and 4 have equal parasite abundance.

Q1:   Do you agree with hypothesis 1? Use data from the table to support your opinion.

. . . .

Q2:   Do you agree with hypothesis 2? Use data from the table to support your opinion.

. . . .

Q3:   Do you agree with hypothesis 3? Use data from the table to support your opinion.

. . . .

8.2   Learning points

> **Summary**
>
> - Some parasites are difficult to culture in the laboratory.
>
> - Rapid parasite antigen change makes designing vaccines extremely difficult.
>
> - The metabolisms of the host and parasite are often very similar, thus making it difficult to develop drugs that target the parasite without harming the host.
>
> - Controlling parasites is easier where civil engineering has resulted in effective sanitation.
>
> - Controlling parasites is difficult in areas of overcrowding, tropical climates, developing countries, refugee camps or areas hit by natural disasters.
>
> - Where parasite control is improving, child mortality is falling. Children have better growth, development and the chance to increase their intelligence.

8.3   Extended response question

The activity which follows presents an extended response question similar to the style that you will encounter in the examination.

You should have a good understanding of the treatment and control of parasites before attempting the question.

You should give your completed answer to your teacher or tutor for marking, or try to mark it yourself using the suggested marking scheme.

Extended response question: The treatment and control of parasites

Discuss the statement that "there are major challenges in the treatment and control of parasites". *(10 marks)*

. . . .

8.4 End of topic test

End of Topic 8 test

Q4: Overcoming parasites can be _____. *(1 mark)*

a) easy
b) difficult

....

Q5: This is because the parasite evolution rate can be _____. *(1 mark)*

a) fast
b) slow

....

Q6: Another factor is that parasites are _____ to culture in the laboratory. *(1 mark)*

a) easy
b) difficult

....

Q7: Additionally, the host and parasite have very _____ metabolisms. *(1 mark)*

a) different
b) similar

....

Q8: What is the main reason that parasite abundance in the UK is so low? *(1 mark)*

....

Q9: Which condition promotes the spread of parasites as a result of overcrowded refugee camps and a lack of good sanitation? *(1 mark)*

a) Natural disasters
b) Tropical climates
c) War

....

Q10: Which condition promotes the spread of parasites due to a large population of vectors? *(1 mark)*

a) Natural disasters
b) Tropical climates
c) War

....

Go online

Q11: Which condition promotes the spread of parasites by limiting the supply of fresh drinking water or damaging sewage works? *(1 mark)*

a) Natural disasters
b) Tropical climates
c) War

....

Q12: Parasites are more abundant in _____ countries. *(1 mark)*

a) developed
b) developing

....

Q13: If parasite levels fall, infant mortality _____. *(1 mark)*

a) decreases
b) increases

....

Q14: If parasite levels fall, children will see _____ growth and development. *(1 mark)*

a) decreased
b) increased

....

....

Topic 9

End of unit test

End of Unit 2 test

Field techniques for biologists

Go online

Q1: What kind of sampling could involve placing a quadrat every 3 metres along a sandy shore? *(1 mark)*

....

Q2: *Dermatoxys veligera* is a roundworm parasite found in the intestinal tract of herbivore vertebrates such as rabbits. Rabbits feed on the flowering plant grass. Which phyla do each of these species belong to? *(1 mark)*

a) *Dermatoxys veligera* - Nematode; Rabbit - Arthropoda; Grass - Gymnosperm
b) *Dermatoxys veligera* - Platyhelminthes; Rabbit - Arthropoda; Grass - Angiosperm
c) *Dermatoxys veligera* - Platyhelminthes; Rabbit - Chordata; Grass - Gymnosperm
d) *Dermatoxys veligera* - Nematode; Rabbit - Chordata; Grass - Angiosperm

....

Q3: Periwinkles are slow moving shelled animals that live on rocky shores. To which phyla do they belong? *(1 mark)*

....

Q4: Periwinkles are suitable for mark and recapture experiments. The formula

$$N = \frac{MC}{R}$$

is used to estimate periwinkle population size following mark and recapture.

- N = population estimate;
- M = number first captured, marked and released;
- C = total number in second capture;
- R = number marked in second capture.

Periwinkles were marked and recaptured on a rocky shore near Creetown in Galloway. The results are shown below.

- Number of periwinkles first captured, marked and released = 100
- Number of marked periwinkles in second capture = 50
- Number of unmarked periwinkles in second capture = 90

Calculate the estimated population of periwinkles on the rocky shore near Creetown. *(1 mark)*

....

Q5: What is the study of animal behaviour called? *(1 mark)*

....

Q6: An ethogram is a list of all the behaviours shown by species. This can be used to produce time budgets for wild species. Measurements taken to produce a time budget include latency, and the _____ and _____ of particular behaviours. *(1 mark)*

....

Q7:   When studying animal behaviour, anthropomorphism must be avoided. Which of the following notes taken by an ethologist while observing a group of young wolf cubs show anthropomorphism? Choose two. *(2 marks)*

A) Wagging their tails.

B) Having fun.

C) Making friends.

D) Barking.

. . . .

Evolution

Q8: Over several generations in a small population the gene pool seemed to change randomly. What process is likely to be responsible? *(1 mark)*

. . . .

Q9: What causes variation in traits to arise in populations? *(1 mark)*

. . . .

Q10: What can mutations be aside from being either beneficial or harmful? *(1 mark)*

. . . .

Q11: In evolutionary theory, fitness can be termed absolute or relative. Which of the following is the correct definition of absolute fitness? *(1 mark)*

a) Frequencies of a particular genotype from one generation to the next.
b) Frequencies of a particular phenotype from one generation to the next.
c) Surviving offspring of one genotype compared with other genotypes.
d) Surviving offspring of one phenotype compared with other phenotypes.

. . . .

Q12: In evolutionary theory, fitness can be termed absolute or relative. Which of the following is the correct definitions of relative fitness? *(1 mark)*

a) Frequencies of a particular genotype from one generation to the next.
b) Frequencies of a particular phenotype from one generation to the next.
c) Surviving offspring of one genotype compared with other genotypes.
d) Surviving offspring of one phenotype compared with other phenotypes.

. . . .

Q13: The rate of evolution can be increased by several factors. Which of the following will increase the rate of evolution? Choose three. *(3 marks)*

A) Cold environments.
B) Horizontal gene transfer.
C) Long generation times.
D) Short generations times.
E) Warm environments.

. . . .

Q14: A change in the traits of one species acting as a selection pressure on another species with which it frequently interacts is called _____. *(1 mark)*

. . . .

Q15: After many generations, tapeworm parasite species evolved hooks to be able to grip onto their human host's intestinal lining. After many subsequent generations, humans evolved to produce an enzyme capable of dislodging the tapeworm's hooks.

What name is given to this evolutionary arms race? *(1 mark)*

. . . .

Variation and sexual reproduction

Q16: Which of the following are true of sexual reproduction? Choose two. *(2 marks)*

A) Horizontal gene transfer in bacteria is an example.

B) Great variation may occur throughout offspring.

C) No variation in offspring.

D) Only half the population is able to produce offspring.

....

Q17: Which of the following is true of asexual reproduction? *(1 mark)*

a) Driving force for the Red Queen's arms race.

b) Great variation in offspring.

c) Only half of the population is able to produce offspring.

d) Vegetative propagation in plants is an example.

....

Q18: In an environment where female komodo dragons struggle to find a male to mate with, what method of asexual reproduction do they use? *(1 mark)*

....

Q19: Which of the following statements about homologous chromosomes is false? *(1 mark)*

a) Each inherited from a different parent.

b) Same centromere position.

c) Same genes at different gene loci.

d) Same size.

....

Q20: When does crossing over occur? *(1 mark)*

a) Meiosis I

b) Meiosis II

....

Q21: When does independent assortment occur? *(1 mark)*

a) Meiosis I

b) Meiosis II

....

Q22: How many cells does meiosis produce? *(1 mark)*

a) 2

b) 4

....

Q23: What kind of cells are produced by meiosis? *(1 mark)*

a) Diploid
b) Haploid

....

Q24: The cells that are produced by meiosis are genetically _____. *(1 mark)*

a) different
b) identical

....

Q25: Male fruit flies have an X and a smaller Y chromosome. What term describes this condition? *(1 mark)*

....

Q26: Genes J, K, L, M and N are all found on the same chromosome. What term is used to describe genes located on the same chromosome? *(1 mark)*

....

Q27: The recombination frequencies of genes J, K, L, M and N are given in the following table.

Genes	Recombination frequency (%)
N and J	16
M and L	6
K and M	27
K and L	33
K and N	4
J and M	7

In which order would these genes appear on the chromosome? *(1 mark)*

....

Q28: The diagram below shows two homologous chromosomes.

Between which of the following alleles would the frequency of recombination be greatest? *(1 mark)*

a) A and B
b) B and D
c) A and D
d) B and C
e) A and C

....

Q29: Many species of snail have both male and female reproductive systems. What term is used to describe this? *(1 mark)*

....

Q30: In some species, the sex of offspring is not controlled by genetic factors. What factors control it in these cases? *(1 mark)*

....

Q31: In fruit flies, males are heterogametic and eye colour is carried on the X chromosome. The allele for red eyes R is dominant to the allele for white eyes r. If the mother had white eyes and the father had red eyes, what will be the appearance of the offspring? *(1 mark)*

a) White eyed females and red eyed males.
b) White eyed females and white eyed males.
c) Red eyed females and white eyed males.
d) Red eyed females and red eyed males.

....

Q32: Red green colour blindness is a recessive human sex-linked trait.   An X chromosome in every cell gets inactivated. Which of the following statements explain why the female does not then show red green colour blindness where the normal allele has been inactivated? Choose two. *(2 marks)*

A) Inactivation is random.

B) At least half of her cells will have a working copy of the gene.

C) Only the chromosome carrying the red green colour blindness allele gets inactivated.

....

Sex and behaviour

Q33: Which of the following correctly identifies the characteristics of sperm and eggs? *(1 mark)*

a) Sperm: many; Eggs: many.
b) Sperm: few; Eggs: contain an energy store.
c) Sperm: contain an energy store; Eggs: few.
d) Sperm: many; Eggs: contain an energy store.

....

Q34: Which sex is considered to make a greater sexual investment? *(1 mark)*

....

Q35: Which of the following statements about parental investment is true? *(1 mark)*

a) In a stable environment, organisms produce many, cheap offspring.
b) r-selected organisms produce many offspring, but provide no parental care.
c) All organisms can be easily classified as either r-selected or K-selected.
d) Organisms inhabiting stable environments will likely have one large reproductive event.

....

Q36: Birds of paradise show distinct differences between males and females. What term is used to describe the differences between males and females? *(1 mark)*

....

Q37: Which of the following potentially increases a male's access to females? Choose three. *(3 marks)*

A) Hunting.
B) Large size.
C) Sneaking.
D) Use of weaponry.

....

Q38: What is the irreversible developmental process that occurs during a critical time period in young birds and may influence mate choice later in life called? *(1 mark)*

....

Q39: What refers to smaller, duller females that tend to camouflage better than males? *(1 mark)*

a) Fitness
b) Inconspicuous
c) Lekking
d) Reversed sexual dimorphism

....

Q40: What refers to females tending to be larger and more conspicuous than males? *(1 mark)*

a) Fitness
b) Inconspicuous
c) Lekking
d) Reversed sexual dimorphism

. . . .

Q41: What is a behaviour shown by male birds and insects, where they display to females in a communal area? *(1 mark)*

a) Fitness
b) Inconspicuous
c) Lekking
d) Reversed sexual dimorphism

. . . .

Q42: What can be assessed by females in terms of good genes and low parasite burden? *(1 mark)*

a) Fitness
b) Inconspicuous
c) Lekking
d) Reversed sexual dimorphism

. . . .

The parasite niche, transmission and virulence

Q43: Which of the following statements are true of parasites? Choose three. *(3 marks)*

A) Wide niche.

B) Narrow niche.

C) High host specificity.

D) Low host specificity.

E) Often lack certain structures and organs.

F) Have a full complement of structures and organs.

. . . .

Q44: Nematodes in the intestines of turtles lack a digestive system and are said to be: *(1 mark)*

a) competitive exclusion.

b) degenerate.

c) fundamental.

d) realised.

e) resource partitioning.

. . . .

Q45: When two species have such similar niches that one becomes locally extinct as a result in interspecific competition, this is known as: *(1 mark)*

a) competitive exclusion

b) degenerate

c) fundamental

d) realised

e) resource partitioning

. . . .

Q46: A species occupies its _____ niche when interspecific competition is absent. *(1 mark)*

a) competitive exclusion

b) degenerate

c) fundamental

d) realised

e) resource partitioning

. . . .

Q47: A species occupies its _____ niche when interspecific competition is present. *(1 mark)*

a) competitive exclusion
b) degenerate
c) fundamental
d) realised
e) resource partitioning

....

Q48: Species participating in interspecific completion may co-exist by: *(1 mark)*

a) competitive exclusion.
b) degenerate.
c) fundamental.
d) realised.
e) resource partitioning.

....

Q49: What name is given to the host in or on which the parasite reaches sexual maturity? *(1 mark)*

....

Q50: Another host is sometimes needed as a vector or for the parasite to complete its life cycle. What name is given to this host? *(1 mark)*

....

Q51: A parasite has the potential to harm its host. What term refers to this? *(1 mark)*

....

Q52: Which statement would be referred to as part of the extended phenotype of a parasite? *(1 mark)*

a) Alteration of host foraging.
b) Similarity to the host cell metabolism.
c) Transmission
d) Virulence

....

Immune response to parasites

Q53: Parasites often _____ the host's immune system. *(1 mark)*

a) promote
b) suppress

....

Q54: Parasites often _____ host size. *(1 mark)*

a) decrease
b) increase

....

Q55: Parasites often _____ host reproduction. *(1 mark)*

a) decrease
b) increase

....

Q56: When the skin becomes wounded, the surrounding area becomes red and warm due to increased blood flow. What name is given to this response? *(1 mark)*

....

Q57: Phagocytosis is a non-specific cellular defence. Arrange the stages in the process of phagocytosis in the correct order. *(1 mark)*

A) Lysosomes fuse with the vacuole.
B) Pathogen is digested by enzymes.
C) Phagocyte engulfs the pathogen into a vacuole.
D) Product of pathogen digestion released into host cell cytoplasm.

....

Q58: B lymphocytes respond to foreign _____ by producing special proteins. *(1 mark)*

a) antibodies
b) antigens
c) apoptosis
d) clonal selection

....

Q59: The special proteins are called: *(1 mark)*

a) antibodies.
b) antigens.
c) apoptosis.
d) clonal selection.

....

Q60: T lymphocytes destroy infected cells by bringing about: *(1 mark)*

a) antibodies.
b) antigens.
c) apoptosis.
d) clonal selection.

....

Q61: During specific responses, lymphocytes become amplified through mitosis. This process is called: *(1 mark)*

a) antibodies.
b) antigens.
c) apoptosis.
d) clonal selection.

....

Q62: It is important to study the outbreak and spread of infectious diseases. What name is given to this field of biology? *(1 mark)*

....

Q63: NHS Scotland advises that all pre-school and primary school children receive the influenza vaccine in order to reduce the spread of influenza, particularly to vulnerable older adults, e.g. grandparents. What is this protection method an example of? *(1 mark)*

....

Parasitic life cycles and viruses

Q64: Schistosomiasis is a human disease caused by Schistosoma: *(1 mark)*

a) flatworms.
b) roundworms.

. . . .

Q65: Another human disease caused by a parasite is malaria. How many hosts does the *Plasmodium* parasite require to complete its life cycle? *(1 mark)*

a) 1
b) 2

. . . .

Q66: Influenza and HIV are both human diseases caused by: *(1 mark)*

a) bacteria.
b) viruses.

. . . .

Q67: Ectoparasitic arthropods, such as ticks, complete their life cycle on one host. Which of the following statements are true of arthropods? Choose three. *(3 marks)*

A) Jointed legs.
B) Contain a shell.
C) Body not divided into segments.
D) Segmented body.
E) Exoskeleton.

. . . .

Q68: Which of the following statements are true of virus structure? Choose three. *(3 marks)*

A) They are surrounded by a protein coat.
B) They contain only DNA.
C) They contain RNA or DNA.
D) They contain only RNA.
E) Some have a lipid membrane surround.
F) All have a lipid membrane surround.

. . . .

Q69: Arrange the steps of the replication of a virus in the correct order. *(1 mark)*

A) Virus uses the host cell's machinery and raw materials to replicate its DNA and synthesise protein coat.

B) Virus injects its DNA into the host cell.

C) These then leave the cell to infect new cells and the host cell undergoes lysis, bursting.

D) Virus interrupts the host cell's own metabolism, often entering the host's genome.

E) Virus attaches to the surface of the host cell.

F) The new DNA then enters the newly formed protein coats, thus producing many new viruses.

....

Q70: Retroviruses contain RNA rather than DNA. On inserting the RNA into the host, it must first be converted into DNA. What enzyme catalyses this reaction? *(1 mark)*

....

Challenges in treatment and control

Q71: Developing countries, such as Malawi, find it more difficult to control parasites than developed countries, such as the UK. Which of the following statements does not explain why this is the case? *(1 mark)*

a) Developing countries usually have tropical climates.
b) Developing countries may have more natural disasters.
c) Developing countries have poor sanitation.
d) Developing countries have higher populations.
e) There are more vectors in developing countries, e.g. mosquitoes.
f) Overcrowding is more common in developing countries.
g) Many developing countries are in conflict.

....

....

Glossary

Absolute fitness

the ratio of frequencies of a particular genotype from one generation to the next

Amoeba

a single-celled parasite

Angiosperms

flowering plants

Anthropomorphism

crediting animal behaviour with human emotions or qualities

Antigen

a protein that may induce an immune response if it is foreign

Antigenic variation

where parasites show great variety amongst different strains

Apoptosis

cell death

Arthropoda

joint-legged invertebrates which are identified by their segmented body, typically with paired appendages, e.g. wasps, butterflies, spiders, and crabs

Autosome

any chromosome that is not a sex chromosome

Bacteriophage

a virus that targets a bacterial host

B lymphocytes

white blood cells that produce specific antibodies in response to specific antigens

Chiasmata

the place where two homologous chromosomes come into contact with one another

Chordata

sea squirts and vertebrates, e.g. birds, mammals, reptiles, amphibians and fish

Civil engineering

a profession that is involved in the design and manufacture of infrastructure to improve standards of living

Clonal selection

lymphocytes become amplified, with some clones used in immediate defence and other clones acting as memory cells

Co-evolution

where a change in the traits of one species acts as a selection pressure on another species with which it frequently interacts

Competitive exclusion principle

when two species are in intense competition with one another and the weaker of the two species becomes locally extinct

Crossing over

the process where homologous chromosomes swap genetic material

Cysticercosis

a parasitic tissue infection

Definitive (primary) host

the host where the parasite reaches sexual maturity

Ectoparasite

a parasite that lives on the surface of the host, e.g. ticks

Endoparasite

a parasite that lives inside the host, e.g. tapeworms and flatworms

Epidemiology

the study of the outbreak and spread of infectious diseases

Ethogram

chart on which observed animal behaviour is recorded

Ethology

study of animal behaviour

Evolution

the change, over successive generations, in the proportion of individuals in a population differing in one or more inherited traits

Extended phenotype

a theory whereby the parasite modifies the host's behaviour to increase its own transmission

Ferns

flowerless plants that reproduce by producing spores and which have a vascular system

Fundamental niche

the niche that an organism occupies when there are no other species present competing for space or resources

Genetic drift

the random change in how frequently a particular allele occurs within a small population

Gravid proglottid

the segment of a tapeworm containing both male and female reproductive organs

Gymnosperms

flowerless vascular plants that produce seeds for reproduction, e.g. the conifer

Herd immunity

protection offered to non-immune members of a population by sufficient numbers immune individuals

Herd immunity threshold

the density of resistant hosts in the population required to prevent an epidemic

Hermaphrodite

an organism with both male and female reproductive organs

Heterogametic

dissimilar sex chromosomes, e.g. mammalian males where the Y chromosome is much smaller than the X chromosome

Homologous chromosomes

chromosomes of the same size, same centromere position and which carry the same genes at the same gene loci

Immune surveillance

white blood cells patrol the body, recognising and destroying foreign pathogens

Imprinting

an irreversible process that occurs within a critical period of young bird development - it can have an impact on mate choice later in life

Independent assortment

takes place during meiosis I when homologous chromosomes pair up and line up along the equator - the final position of one pair is completely random relative to every other pair

Inflammatory response

injured or wounded areas become warm and red due to increased blood flow, bringing white cells for defence

Intermediate (secondary) host

the host that the parasite might require in order to complete its life cycle or as a means of transmission, thus making it a vector

Interphase

takes place at the start of meiosis when DNA replication occurs

K-selected

larger organisms that usually produce lower numbers of offspring, providing more extensive parental care and have longer life spans

Lekking

males display for females in a communal display area, then females choose a mate

Line transect

line along which quadrats are placed or samples taken

Linked genes

genes that are on the same chromosome

Liverworts

flowerless, spore producing plants with flattened stems and overlapping leaves

Lysis

the bursting of a host cell, releasing many virus particles

Malaria

a serious human disease spread by mosquitoes that are infected with the malaria parasite

Meiosis

a special type of cell division where four haploid gametes are produced from one diploid gamete mother cell

Memory cells

cloned lymphocytes that remain in the body to respond faster if the individual is exposed to the same antigen a second time

Mollusca

molluscs which are greatly varied, with many characterised by the presence of a shell, e.g. snails and octopi

Monogamy

where animals form breeding pairs, thus one male to one female

Mosses

flowerless plants, lacking seeds and a vascular system

Mutation

random change in DNA sequences within a population

Mutualism

symbiotic relationship where both species benefit

Natural killer cells

lymphocytes responsible for destroying abnormal cells

Natural selection

non-random process whereby certain alleles occur more frequently within a population because they confer a selective advantage

Nematoda

round worms. which show great variety, many of which are parasitic, e.g. tapeworms

Parasite

an organism that gains food and shelter at the expense of the host

Parthenogenesis

asexual reproduction whereby embryos develop from an unfertilised egg

Phagocyte

white blood cell in non-specific defence, engulfing and destroying foreign antigens -may also present antigens to lymphocytes

Phagocytosis

non-specific defence where phagocytes engulf foreign antigens and digest them using digestive enzymes present in lysosomes

Platyhelminthes

flatworms which show bilateral symmetry with internal organs present, but which lack a body cavity, many of which are parasitic

Point count

sampling techniques used for birds

Pollinator

an organism that transfers pollen from the anther of one flower to the stigma of usually another flower, e.g. bee or hummingbird

Polygamy

usually where one male has access to mate with several females

Random sampling

individuals selected from the larger population must be chosen completely by chance

Realised niche

the niche that an organism occupies when there is competition from other species

Recombinant

the chromosome created when linked genes are separated during crossing over

Red Queen hypothesis

a theory concerning co-evolution of a parasite and its host

Relative fitness

the ratio of surviving offspring of one genotype compared with other genotypes

Resource partitioning

where two species occupy different realised niches, allowing them to co-exist by compromising over resources

Retrotransposon

the piece of DNA that carries out reverse transcription before being inserted into a new site on the genome

Retrovirus

a virus that contains RNA as its nucleic acid

Reverse transcriptase

an enzyme used by retroviruses to synthesise DNA that can be inserted into the host cell's genome

r-selected

smaller organisms that usually produce larger numbers of offspring, providing no parental care and having shorter life spans

Sanitation

access to facilities for safely disposing of human waste such as urine and faeces

Satellite male

male that sneaks to gain access to females

Schistosomiasis

also known as bilharzias, a human disease caused by parasites living in fresh water in sub-tropical and tropical regions of the world

Sessile

organism that is fixed in position - cannot move

Sexual dimorphism

physical difference between males and females of a species

Sexual selection

a non-random process, whereby certain alleles occur more frequently within a population because they are selected/preferred by one sex

Sneaker

male that gains access to mate with females without the more dominant male knowing

Stratified sampling

individuals are randomly selected from sub-groups within a population

Symbiosis

an interrelationship between organisms of two different species, whereby at least one species benefits

Systematic sampling

where samples may be taken at regular/pre-set intervals, e.g. every 2m along the transect

Taxonomy

grouping living organisms based on similarities or relatedness

Terrain

the physical geography of the land

T lymphocytes

lymphocytes that destroy specific infected or damaged cells by bringing about apoptosis

Transmission

the spread of a parasite to a host

Vector

the means of transmitting a parasite

Vegetative propagation/cloning

a form of asexual reproduction that takes place in some plants, resulting in offspring that are genetically identical to the parent plant, e.g. bulbs and runners

Virulence

the deleterious effect that the parasite has on the host

Waterborne

transmitted by water

Answers to questions and activities

1 Field techniques for biologists

Sampling of wild organisms: Questions (page 4)

Q1: 92

Q2: 96

Q3: Samples were taken every 3 m / at regular intervals.

Identification and taxonomy: Activity (page 11)

Q4:

Angiosperm:	flowering plants.
Anthropods:	invertebrates with jointed pairs of legs and segmented bodies.
Chordata:	animal group containing sea squirts and vertebrates.
Fern:	flowerless plant that produces spores and has a vascular system.
Gymnosperm:	non-flowering, seed producing vascular plant such as a conifer.
Moss:	flowerless plant, lacking both seeds and a vascular system.
Molluscs:	invertebrate group often found to have a shell.
Nematodes:	parasitic roundworms.
Platyhelminthes:	parasitic flatworms.

Monitoring populations: Question (page 12)

Q5: 2160

Measuring and recording animal behaviour: Question (page 14)

Q6: B and D.

B. Offspring *begged* mother for food.
D. Offspring *smiled* at mother.

End of Topic 1 test (page 16)

Q7: Any two from:

- isolation;
- terrain;
- tidal changes;
- weather conditions.

Q8: Any from:

- camera traps;
- remote detection;
- scat sampling.

Q9: c) 10 pupils from each year group in a school are randomly selected and their pulse rate is taken.

Q10: b) Nematode: Parasitic roundworm; Angiosperm: Flowering plant

Q11: Any two from:

- banding;
- hair clipping;
- painting;
- surgical implantation;
- tagging.

Q12: 500

Q13: Ethology

Q14: An ethogram

Q15: a) Anthropomorphism

2 Evolution

Drift and selection: Questions (page 21)

Q1: a) Genetic drift

Q2: b) Natural or sexual selection

Q3: b) Natural or sexual selection

Q4: a) Genetic drift

Q5: The ratio of frequencies of a particular genotype from one generation to the next is defined as **absolute** fitness.

Q6: The ratio of surviving offspring of one genotype compared with other genotypes is defined as **relative** fitness.

Rate of evolution: Questions (page 23)

Q7: d) 1 and 2

Q8: a) Numbers decrease

Q9: Effectiveness would decrease as the *Staphylococcus aureas* will evolve resistance quickly due to a short generation time and horizontal gene transfer.

Co-evolution and the Red Queen: Questions (page 31)

Q10: 112.5 %

Q11: Number of nematodes in slug population 2 never increases higher than 25 in comparison to 450 in population 1.

Q12: Random mutation, resulting in resistance. Resistant individuals are more likely to reproduce so the resistance gene becomes more frequent in subsequent generations.

Q13: Nematode numbers would increase OR slug numbers would decrease.

End of Topic 2 test (page 33)

Q14: Genetic drift

Q15: Mutation

Q16: Relative

Q17: Warm environment, Shorter generation time, Horizontal gene transfer

Q18: Horizontal gene transfer and shorter generation times.

Q19: b) Hosts

Q20: a) Herbivores

Q21: b) Plants

Q22: c) Prey

Q23: Red Queen

3 Variation and sexual reproduction

Costs and benefits of reproduction: Questions (page 40)

Q1: c) 4

Q2: c) Vegetative propagation

Q3: b) Parthenogenesis

Q4: a) Horizontal gene transfer

Meiosis forms variable gametes: Activity (page 44)

Q5:

1. Chromosomes undergo DNA replication (interphase).
2. Homologous chromosomes line up at the equator of the cell.
3. Homologous chromosomes touch at points called chiasmata.
4. Crossing over occurs at points called chiasmata.
5. Independent assortment occurs.
6. Two haploid cells are formed.
7. Chromatids are separated by spindle fibres.
8. Four haploid gametes are produced.

Meiosis forms variable gametes: Questions (page 44)

Q6: 6

Q7: 3

Q8: 8

Q9: LCPB or BPCL as per the following diagram:

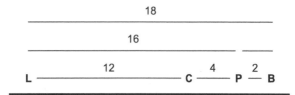

Sex determination: Questions (page 48)

Q10: 20 %

Q11: 10 %

Q12: 240

Q13: 540

Q14: 50 %

Q15: 50 %

Q16: 50 %

Extended response question: Meiosis (page 50)

Suggested marking scheme

Each line represents a point worth one mark. The concept may be expressed in other words. Words which are bracketed are not essential. Alternative answers are separated by a solidus (/); if both such answers are given, only a single mark is allocated. In checking the answer, the number of the point being allocated a mark should be written on the answer paper. A maximum of ten marks can be gained. A maximum of three marks can be gained from points 5-8.

1. Meiosis produces four haploid gametes...

2. ...from one diploid gamete mother cell.

3. Interphase is where DNA replications occurs.

4. During meiosis I, homologous chromosomes line up at the equator of the cell.

5. Homologous chromosomes are the same size and shape.

6. They carry the same genes at same gene loci...

7. ...but may carry different alleles / one from each parent.

8. They have their centromere at the same place.

9. During meiosis I, crossing over may occur...

10. ...at points called chiasmata.

11. This process shuffles sections of DNA between the homologous pairs, allowing the recombination of alleles to occur thus increasing variation.

12. Genes on the same chromosome are said to be linked.

13. There is a correlation between the distance between linked genes and their frequency of recombination / description or definition of chromosome mapping.

14. Independent assortment occurs as a result of meiosis I, with homologous chromosomes being separated irrespective of their maternal and paternal origin.

15. Homologous chromosomes are separated by spindle fibres.

16. This increases variation in the gametes.

17. During meiosis II, chromatids are pulled apart (and four haploid gametes are produced).

End of Topic 3 test (page 50)

Q17: c) Only half of each parent's genome is passed onto offspring.

Q18: b) increasing

Q19: b) This is common in plants.

Q20: A, B and C.

A) Crossing over occurs at points called chiasmata.

B) Independent assortment occurs.

C) Homologous chromosomes are separated.

Q21: Any two from:

- same size;
- same centromere position;
- same genes at same gene loci;
- alleles may differ due to different parental origin.

Q22: Independent assortment and crossing over.

Q23: linked

Q24: Hermaphrodite

Q25: a) Heterogametic

Q26: a) one copy

Q27: b) two copies

Q28: Random inactivation of parts of the X chromosome OR half of the cells in any tissue will have a working copy of the gene.

4 Sex and behaviour

Sexual investment: Activity (page 60)

Q1:

Characteristic	r-selected population	K-selected population
Environment	Unstable	Stable
Lifespan	Short	Long
Number of offspring per reproductive episode	Many	Few
Number of reproductions in lifetime	Usually one	Often several
Size of offspring or eggs	Small	Large
Parental care	None	Often extensive

Courtship: Questions (page 65)

Q2: c) sexual dimorphism.

Q3: b) lekking.

Q4: d) sneaking behaviour.

Q5: a) imprinting.

Q6:

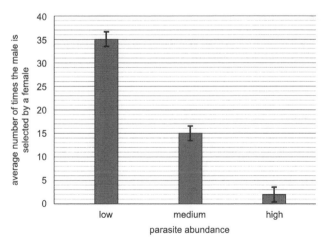

Q7: 57.1 %

Q8: The higher the parasite abundance the lower the mating success.

Q9: Low parasite abundance suggests that the male may have good parasite or disease resistant genes. These are 'honest' signals.

Extended response question: Courtship (page 68)

Suggested marking scheme

Each line represents a point worth one mark. The concept may be expressed in other words. Words which are bracketed are not essential. Alternative answers are separated by a solidus (/); if both such answers are given, only a single mark is allocated. In checking the answer, the number of the point being allocated a mark should be written on the answer paper. A maximum of ten marks can be gained.

Sexual diamorphism (maximum of 4 marks):

1. Sexual dimorphism is the physical difference between males and females of the same species.

2. Usually, males are more conspicuous than females / a suitable description.

3. Being inconspicuous mean that females can better protect their young due to camouflage.

4. Sexual dimorphism is a product of sexual selection.

5. Sexual dimorphism can be reversed in some species.

Male-male rivalry (maximum of 1 mark):

i   Males often use large size to out compete other smaller males for mates.

ii Some males use weaponry to win females / suitable description of horns or antlers.

Sneakers (1 mark):

I   Smaller males may still be successful using sneaker / satellite behaviour.

Lekking (maximum of 4 marks):

a) Lekking is where males collect in a display area and present to females.

b) The display area is called a lek.

c) A suitable example, e.g. grouse, capercaillie.

d) Females assess male fitness...

e) ...and choose based on 'honest' signals...

f) ...such as low parasite burden.

End of Topic 4 test (page 68)

Q10: b) greater than

Q11: A and C
A. Hermaphrodism
C. Long sex organs

Q12: c) Production of many offspring, short life spans, no parental care.

Q13: Sexual dimorphism

Q14: b) To provide better camouflage when protecting their young.

Q15: Sneaking behaviour

Q16: c) Irreversible, occurs within a critical period, can have an effect on choice of mate.

5 The parasite niche, transmission and virulence

The parasite niche: Activity (page 77)

Q1:

Fundamental niche:	exists in the absence of interspecific competition.
Realised niche:	exists in the presence of interspecific competition.
Resource partitioning:	two different species compromise over resources to reduce competition.
Competitive exclusion principle:	competition between two species will see local extinction of the weaker.
Vector:	responsible for parasite transmission.
Definitive host:	where the parasite reaches sexual maturity.
Intermediate host:	required by some parasites to complete their life cycle.

Transmission and virulence: Questions (page 79)

Q2: 157.1 %

Q3: b) 2011

Q4: c) 2012

Q5: Rabbits are an intermediate host so their greater numbers increased their role as a vector.
OR
The fox population increased due to food availability and parasite transmission increased due to overcrowding.

Extended response question: Parasite niche (page 81)

Suggested marking scheme

Each line represents a point worth one mark. The concept may be expressed in other words. Words which are bracketed are not essential. Alternative answers are separated by a solidus (/); if both such answers are given, only a single mark is allocated. In checking the answer, the number of the point being allocated a mark should be written on the answer paper. A maximum of ten marks can be gained.

1. Parasites and hosts have a symbiotic relationship. . .

2. . . .that benefits the parasite at the expense of the host.

3. Parasite niche is a complex summary of tolerances and needs.

4. Parasites have narrow niche due to high host specificity.

5. Parasites are defined as degenerate due to loss of certain organs or structures.

6. Fundamental niche is the niche that exists in the absence of interspecific competition.

7. Realised niche is the niche that exists in the presence of interspecific competition.

8. Interspecific competition will result when two species have very similar niches.

9. Interspecific competition can lead to competitive exclusion principle, which is local extinction of one (the weaker) of the two competing species.

10. Resource partitioning allows two species to co-exist (by compromising).

11. Endoparasites live inside the host and ectoparasites live on the surface of the host.

12. A definitive host is the host where the parasite reaches sexual maturity.

13. An intermediate host may be a vector and is needed for the parasite to complete its life cycle.

14. Vectors have a role in parasite transmission from one host to another. . .

15. . . .such as the mosquito spreading the malaria parasite / any other suitable example of a vector.

End of Topic 5 test (page 81)

Q6: a) benefit

Q7: b) detriment

Q8: a) narrow

Q9: a) high

Q10: Degenerate

Q11: Intermediate OR secondary host

Q12: Definitive OR primary host

Q13: Competitive exclusion principle

Q14: Resource partitioning

Q15: B and C
B. The nematode *Acsaris* inhabits the first 20% of the human intestine and the nematode *Strongyloides* inhabits the last 20% of the human intestine.
C. The mouse parasite *Heligmosomoides polygyrus* is suited to the acidic pH of the stomach, whereas the parasite *Litomosoides sigmodontis* has adapted to the more neutral pH of the small intestine.

Q16: b) Modification of host behaviour

6 Immune response to parasites

Non-specific defence: Activity (page 86)

Q1:

1. Phagocytes move to the site of injury.
2. Plasma membrane of the phagocyte engulfs the parasite.
3. Parasite is brought into the phagocyte in a vacuole.
4. Lysosomes move towards the vacuole.
5. Lysosomes fuse with the vacuole releasing digestive enzymes.
6. The parasite is digested.

Specific defence: Questions (page 91)

Q2:

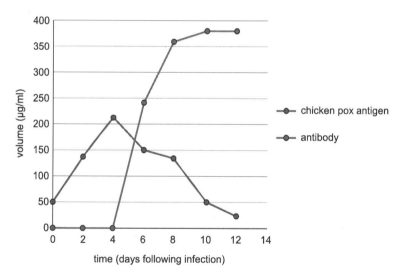

Q3: The volume of chicken pox antigen starts at 50μg/ml on day 0 (day of infection). This rises to a maximum volume of 220μg/ml 4 days following infection. The volume of chicken pox antigen then falls eventually to 20μg/ml 12 days following infection. (*units needed at least once*)

Q4: The volume of antibody remains at 0μg/ml from day 0 to 4 days following infection. This then increases to 240μg/ml 6 days following infection. This increases to 380μg/ml by 10 days following infection, where it remains steady to 12 days following infection. (*units needed at least once*)

Q5:   Volume of chicken pox antigen falls quickly from 50μg/ml on day 0 to 0μg/ml 2 days following infection. This is because the volume of antibody increases rapidly to 240μg/ml 2 days following infection. By 6 days following infection the volume of antibody is at a maximum of 400μg/ml. This rapid secondary response is the result of clonal selection that occurred in the first chicken pox response and the immunological memory cells present in the individual.

Extended response question: Immune responses (page 94)

Suggested marking scheme

Each line represents a point worth one mark. The concept may be expressed in other words. Words which are bracketed are not essential. Alternative answers are separated by a solidus (/); if both such answers are given, only a single mark is allocated. In checking the answer, the number of the point being allocated a mark should be written on the answer paper. A maximum of ten marks can be gained.

1. Defences can be non-specific / natural *and* specific / adaptive.

2. Physical barriers such as the skin prevent entry of parasites.

3. Chemical secretions such as mucus, tears, saliva and stomach acid.

4. Inflammatory response increases bloodflow and therefore phagocytes to site of injury or parasite.

5. Natural killer cells destroy *abnormal* cells.

6. Phagocytosis is where phagocytes engulf parasites into a vacuole/vesicle. . .

7. . . .and digestive enzymes in lysosomes digest the parasite.

8. White cells carry out 'surveillance'.

9. Phagocytes display foreign antigens to lymphocytes.

10. A specific lymphocyte is produced in response to each foreign antigen.

11. Lymphocytes undergo mitosis so are amplified.

12. This is called clonal selection.

13. T cells / T lymphocytes target infected or damaged cells.

14. T cells induce apoptosis (cell death).

15. B cells / B lymphocytes produce specific antibodies to specific antigens.

16. Some cloned lymphocytes act as immunological memory cells.

End of Topic 6 test (page 94)

Q6:

Non-specific defence	Specific defence
Inflammatory response	Action by B cells
Mucus	Action by T cells
Phagocytosis	Clonal selection
Skin	Phagocytes present antigens

Q7: During phagocytosis, special organelles release digestive **enzymes** into the vacuole containing the parasite.

Q8: Lysosomes

Q9: Clonal selection

Q10: d) apoptosis of specific damaged cells.

Q11: a) Mimics host antigens.

Q12: b) will not

Q13: Herd or community immunity

Q14: Epidemiology

7 Parasitic life cycles and viruses

Parasitic life cycles: Questions (page 103)

Q1: b) False

Q2: single-celled

Q3: a) True

Q4: -

Q5: b) False

Q6: flatworms

Q7: b) False

Q8: vectors

Q9: b) *Plasmodium.*

Q10: c) *Schistosoma.*

Q11: a) an arthropod tick.

Q12: Endoparasite

Q13: Human and tsetse fly.

Q14: The variant surface glycoproteins do not allow the immune system / white blood cells / antibodies to attach to fight or render the parasite harmless.

Q15: Antigenic variation means that one medicine / vaccine will not be suitable for all variants.

Replication of a retrovirus: Activity (page 108)

Q16:

RNA	→	DNA	→	RNA
-	viral reverse transcriptase	-	host RNA polymerase	-

End of Topic 7 test (page 110)

Q17: Any four from:

- protists;
- platyhelminthes;
- nematodes;
- arthropods;
- bacteria;
- viruses.

Q18: a) direct

Q19: b) indirect

Q20: a) secondary hosts.

Q21: b) vectors.

Q22: Malaria and schistosomiasis.

Q23: Bacteria

Q24: Viruses

Q25: a) nm

Q26: 2, 4 and 5

- Lipid coat
- Protein coat
- RNA

Q27: 2 and 4

- They are composed of the host's materials.
- They help the virus remain undetected.

Q28: Reverse transcriptase

Q29: E, B, D, A, F, C

- Virus attaches to the surface of the host cell.
- Virus injects its DNA into the host cell.
- Virus interrupts the host cell's own metabolism, often entering the host's genome.
- Virus uses the host cell's machinery and raw materials to replicate its DNA and synthesise protein coat.
- The new DNA then enters the newly formed protein coats, thus producing many new viruses.
- These then leave the cell to infect new cells and the host cell undergoes lysis, bursting.

8 Challenges in treatment and control

Challenges in treatment and control: Questions (page 115)

Q1: Disagree - parasite abundance will be high, but country 3 will be higher. The population density may produce overcrowding and the sub-tropical climate will promote vector populations; however, with recent improvements in sanitation, parasite abundance should be falling. The hurricane season may cause sanitation problems and increase the chance of parasite abundance.

Q2: Agree - excellent sanitation, temperate climate and no overcrowding are perfect conditions for controlling parasites.

Q3: Disagree - country 3 will have much higher parasite abundance due to overcrowding and poor sanitation, compared with country 4 which has lower population density and increased education, promoting good sanitation. Climates are similar and may promote vectors, but country 4 is in a better state to cope.

Extended response question: The treatment and control of parasites (page 116)

Suggested marking scheme

Each line represents a point worth one mark. The concept may be expressed in other words. Words which are bracketed are not essential. Alternative answers are separated by a solidus (/); if both such answers are given, only a single mark is allocated. In checking the answer, the number of the point being allocated a mark should be written on the answer paper. A maximum of ten marks can be gained. Only two points from 10-13 can be used to gain marks.

1. Parasites are difficult to culture in the laboratory.

2. Many parasites have rapid evolution rates...

3. ...resulting in rapid antigen change.

4. This makes development of vaccines difficult.

5. Developing suitable drugs is also very difficult...

6. ...due to the metabolism of the parasite and their host being so similar...

7. ...since a drug intended to kill a parasite may also harm the host.

8. Control has been noted in areas with improved sanitation / civil engineering / sewage systems.

9. Where vectors are under control parasites are controlled too.

10. Control is particularly difficult in tropical climates / developing countries, ...

11. ...places where there is war / refugee camps, ...

12. ...areas facing natural disasters...

13. . . .and overcrowded regions.

14. Improving parasite control reduces child mortality.

15. Where there are improvements, children are likely to thrive / increase in child growth, development and intelligence.

16. As children develop / become educated, they can continue improving control methods in these countries.

End of Topic 8 test (page 117)

Q4: b) difficult

Q5: a) fast

Q6: b) difficult

Q7: b) similar

Q8: (Civil engineering leading to) good sanitation.

Q9: c) War

Q10: b) Tropical climates

Q11: a) Natural disasters

Q12: b) developing

Q13: a) decreases

Q14: b) increased

9 End of unit test

End of Unit 2 test (page 120)

Q1: Systematic

Q2: d) *Dermatoxys veligera* - Nematode; Rabbit - Chordata; Grass - Angiosperm

Q3: Mollusc

Q4: 280

Q5: Ethology

Q6: An ethogram is a list of all the behaviours shown by species. This can be used to produce time budgets for wild species. Measurements taken to produce a time budget include latency, and the **duration** and **frequency** of particular behaviours.

Q7: B and C

- Having fun.
- Making friends.

Q8: Genetic drift

Q9: Mutation

Q10: Neutral

Q11: a) Frequencies of a particular genotype from one generation to the next.

Q12: c) Surviving offspring of one genotype compared with other genotypes.

Q13: B, D, E

- Horizontal gene transfer.
- Short generations times.
- Warm environments.

Q14: co-evolution

Q15: Red Queen hypothesis

Q16: B and D

- Great variation may occur throughout offspring.
- Only half the population is able to produce offspring.

Q17: d) Vegetative propagation in plants is an example.

Q18: Parthenogenesis

Q19: c) Same genes at different gene loci.

Q20: a) Meiosis I

Q21: a) Meiosis I

Q22: b) 4

Q23: b) Haploid

Q24: a) different

Q25: Heterogametic

Q26: Linked

Q27: KNJML or LMJNK

Q28: c) A and D

Q29: Hermaphroditic

Q30: Environmental

Q31: c) Red eyed females and white eyed males.

Q32: A and B

- Inactivation is random.
- At least half of her cells will have a working copy of the gene.

Q33: d) Sperm: many; Eggs: contain an energy store.

Q34: Female

Q35: b) r-selected organisms produce many offspring, but provide no parental care.

Q36: Sexual dimorphism

Q37: B, C and D

- Large size.
- Sneaking.
- Use of weaponry.

Q38: Imprinting

Q39: b) Inconspicuous

Q40: d) Reversed sexual dimorphism

Q41: c) Lekking

Q42: a) Fitness

Q43: B, C and E

- Narrow niche.
- High host specificity.

- Often lack certain structures and organs.

Q44: b) degenerate.

Q45: a) competitive exclusion

Q46: c) fundamental

Q47: d) realised

Q48: e) resource partitioning.

Q49: Definitive (host)

Q50: Intermediate (host)

Q51: Virulence

Q52: a) Alteration of host foraging.

Q53: b) suppress

Q54: b) increase

Q55: a) decrease

Q56: Inflammatory (response)

Q57: C, A, B, D

- Phagocyte engulfs the pathogen into a vacuole.
- Lysosomes fuse with the vacuole.
- Pathogen is digested by enzymes.
- Product of pathogen digestion released into host cell cytoplasm.

Q58: b) antigens

Q59: a) antibodies.

Q60: c) apoptosis.

Q61: d) clonal selection.

Q62: Epidemiology

Q63: Herd immunity

Q64: a) flatworms.

Q65: b) 2

Q66: b) viruses.

Q67: A, D, E

- Jointed legs.

- Segmented body.
- Exoskeleton.

Q68: A, C, E

- They are surrounded by a protein coat.
- They contain RNA or DNA.
- Some have a lipid membrane surround.

Q69: E, B, D, A, F, C

- Virus attaches to the surface of the host cell.
- Virus injects its DNA into the host cell.
- Virus interrupts the host cell's own metabolism, often entering the host's genome.
- Virus uses the host cell's machinery and raw materials to replicate its DNA and synthesise protein coat.
- The new DNA then enters the newly formed protein coats, thus producing many new viruses.
- These then leave the cell to infect new cells and the host cell undergoes lysis, bursting.

Q70: Reverse transcriptase

Q71: d) Developing countries have higher populations.